PREGNANCY

DaRn
GOOD
AdVicE
PREGNANCY

Susan Warhus MD
Illustrated by David Hitch

MQP

MQ Publications Limited
12 The Ivories, 6–8 Northampton Street
London N1 2HY
Tel: +44 (0) 20 7359 2244
Fax: +44 (0) 20 7359 1616
email: mail@mqpublications.com

North American Office:
49 West 24th Street
New York, NY 10010, USA
Tel: 212-223-6320
email: information@mqpublicationsus.com

website: www.mqpublications.com

Design: **Balley Design Associates**

ISBN: 1-84072-883-3

Printed in Italy
9 8 7 6 5 4 3 2 1

Contents

Preface

So, you're having a baby. What an exciting time in your life! If you are like most women, your emotions are running wild—you're excited, scared, happy, and concerned all at the same time. You've also started to notice some changes in your body. These are perfectly normal experiences as you begin this amazing milestone in your life. The fact that you have begun to read this book shows that you are concerned about your pregnancy and want to understand what is happening to your body. Good for you! You are going to be a caring, terrific mother!

Pregnancy is certainly a time of change and excitement. But this need not be a daunting or stressful time. In fact, this book has been designed to answer your questions and ease your concerns. Of course, we encourage you to see your physician or midwife for your routine prenatal care visits. But sometimes your healthcare provider seems too busy to address all your questions. Keep this book on hand, 24/7, to guide and reassure you.

You can expect to find answers to most of your pregnancy concerns in this book. For example, the book addresses lifestyle changes including diet and exercise. Important prenatal tests are also discussed. There's an entire section that helps you to deal with common aches and pains during pregnancy. When it comes time for delivery, you'll have already read about heading to the hospital and what to expect. There's even a section for dads-to-be. Equally important, there's a chapter devoted to how you might feel after you've delivered your baby.

As a mother myself, I understand the wonder of childbirth and babies. As a physician, I've been very fortunate to assist mothers during their pregnancy and childbirth experience. For me, it's the best part of being a doctor. The joy of delivering a beautiful baby is indescribable. Placing the newborn on Mother's belly, helping Dad cut the umbilical cord, watching the new mother and father beam with happiness and pride—what a privilege to be a part of such a magical event.

I'm delighted to present this book, *Darn Good Advice: Pregnancy* for all expecting mothers-to-be. It emphasizes all of the important need-to-know facts about pregnancy and childbirth. You'll find that it's easy and enjoyable to read because it's written in an amusing, entertaining format.

About the author

Susan Warhus, M.D., is a physician and a board-certified obstetrician and gynecologist. She co-founded the largest all-female practice in Arizona. During her clinical practice, she had the pleasure of delivering more than 3,000 babies.

Dr. Warhus serves on the advisory board for Childbirth Graphics, the largest U.S. childbirth education product company. She is associated with Prepared Childbirth Educators and My Local Pregnancy organizations. She also contributes articles to various women's magazines and makes occasional radio and television appearances. Dr. Warhus is a member of the American College of Obstetricians and Gynecologists and also a member of the American Medical Association.

Throughout this book, when referring to the infant or child, I have tried to alternate the use of "he" and "she" by chapter. This has been done to avoid the impersonal "it" or the sometimes awkward use of the plural form. No gender bias is intended by this writing style.

ChApTeR 1
LeTtInG iT ALL sInK iN

I caN't BeLiEvE iT

Okay, confess! How many home pregnancy test kits have you gone through? Two? Four? More? Does anyone get tested at the doctor's office these days? Just about every new "mom-to be" (yes, that's you now!) buys a bundle of test kits and keeps peeing on that stick over and over until she gets the results she wants. Maybe you just absolutely can't believe that faint blue line and need to do a reassuring check each morning in the early weeks. No wonder companies sell them in two-packs and in bulk through the Internet.

How do the tests work?

There are many types of home pregnancy test kits. Some give you lines to interpret, some colors, some plus and minus signs. Others seem to come out shouting "yes, you are pregnant" or "no, you are not pregnant." They all work in basically the same way—by detecting the presence of a pregnancy hormone called HCG (human chorionic gonadotropin) in your urine. Some home tests are as accurate as those your doctor uses (they might even be the same ones). And most can detect the presence of the pregnancy hormone in your urine within a week or so of conception. That's before you've even missed a period.

Fascinating fact

Fifty years ago, doctors couldn't confirm you were pregnant until they heard the fetal heartbeat with their stethoscope. Pregnant women were usually five months along by that time. I remember my mother telling me how her doctor officially announced she was pregnant when she was about five or six months along. She smiled sweetly, and told him she'd already figured that one out.

top*ten*

...signs of pregnancy

In case you still have doubts about being pregnant, here's a checklist of early pregnancy symptoms. Not everyone experiences them, but you're in good company if you do.

1. Missed period	**6.** Headaches
2. Tender breasts	**7.** Increased sense of smell
3. Nausea	**8.** Constipation
4. Tiredness and fatigue	**9.** Light-headedness
5. Frequent urination	**10.** Heartburn

real life pregnancy

"It was all an accident!"

"We found out I was pregnant on Christmas Eve. It made for an exciting holiday, but we weren't really planning on getting pregnant; it just happened. We had thought of waiting until we had a house and were in a better financial situation. It's still sort of stressful, but our families have promised to help out. I think we'll do just fine."

Jen, age 25

Letting it all sink in **11**

Calculating the big Day

Figuring out when a baby is due is usually a big deal. You have to think back to the most recent times you had sex and try to figure out which occasion might have been THE time. This may involve a lot of concentration and counting.

How do I work it out?

It's easier to figure out when you got pregnant if you are in tune with your menstrual cycle. It's always a good idea to keep track of your periods when trying to conceive (and when trying NOT to conceive). You can check your most fertile days of the month by following the steps below. Of course, there may be variations. Some people have cycles a little shorter or longer than 28 days. Medication, stress, or physical illness may make your hormones a little less predictable. And even if you ovulate (release an egg from one of your ovaries) on day 14, that egg can survive 24 to 36 hours and could be fertilized at any time during this period. What's more, sperm can survive for up to five days. Most have much shorter lives, but it's technically possible to have sex several days before you ovulate and still get pregnant!

Finding your most fertile time

With more couples using natural family planning and the advent of ovulation-predictor kits, many women are aware of their date of ovulation and conception. If that's too much for you, try this easy guide to your most likely time for conception.

1. If you have a regular and predictable menstrual cycle, you probably get a period every 28 days or so. Count the first day of your period as day 1.

2. Keep counting until you reach day 14. This day is classically the most fertile in your cycle.

Mythbusting

The myth: You will deliver your baby exactly on your due date.

The truth: After all the calculating and anticipating of the big event, only 4 percent of women actually deliver on their due date. Most women deliver any time from two weeks before to two weeks after the planned date.

COUNtInG iN wEeKs AnD mOnThS

To add to the confusion about due dates, the medical community counts the length of pregnancy in a different way than the rest of the world. (It's a doctor thing.) For your entire life, you've heard that pregnancy lasts nine months. So, to find your due date you just figure out when you conceived and add nine months, right? Wrong! Forget everything you heard in the movies and from well-meaning friends and family. The medical community doesn't even talk in months; they use *weeks*. And here's the big surprise—40 weeks is normal for a regular term pregnancy or sometimes a range is given of 38 to 42 weeks.

How they do they count it?

To calculate your due date, your doctor or midwife takes the first day of your last period (day 1 on your menstrual calendar) and adds 40 weeks. The assumption is made that you ovulate and conceive approximately two weeks after the first day of your menstrual cycle. Thus, you are due about 38 weeks after conception. In any case, it's no wonder so many women have lively "discussions" with their doctors and midwives about their due date. There is actually some logic and understanding to this method of calculating your due date. The system has been around for quite some time and estimates the due date fairly accurately. And most of us have a better chance of knowing when our last period started than when we actually ovulated (or conceived). If you can't remember when your last period started, an ultrasound performed early in pregnancy can be quite accurate in pinpointing the baby's due date.

Simple math

Here's another easy way to calculate your due date.

1. Add seven days to the first date of your last period.

2. Now add nine months. For example, if the first day of your last period was July 20, add seven days (July 27) and then add nine months, making a due date of April 27.

Fascinating fact

Does 40 weeks seems like a long time to be pregnant? Be thankful you're not a female elephant: In general, the larger the animal, the longer the pregnancy. Here are the average gestational times for some other mammals:

Elephant	95 weeks
Whale	52 weeks
Sea lion	52 weeks
Horse	47 weeks

CHOOSING YOUR DOCTOR OR MIDWIFE

Selecting a doctor or midwife to guide you through pregnancy is a big deal. One of the best ways to find a great healthcare provider is through word of mouth. Ask friends, family, and neighbors for recommendations. It goes without saying that your pregnancy care providers should be educated, trained, and competent. (And, when choosing a midwife, that she has a back-up physician available in case of a complication or emergency). But it's also important that you connect with your healthcare provider as a person. Not only should you feel comfortable enough with him or her to discuss intimate areas of your anatomy and what may seem

to be silly fears (I drank a cup of coffee—did I harm my baby?), you may want a shoulder to sob on (blame the hormones), and a hand to bite during labor. A good doctor or midwife will be willing to provide all this and more to set your mind at ease. And if they can't comply with all your plans and wishes, they should be able to supply the reasons in detail . . . because you're worth it!

Is your medical team like an automobile?

- Classy, admired, and well-respected by others.
- Affordable, covered by your insurance, and within your budget.
- Extremely dependable, trustworthy, and reliable.
- Able to guide you and keep you safe in times of stormy weather.
- Possesses a soft and lush interior, where you can feel cozy, safe, and at home.
- Doesn't break down when the going gets a little tough.
- Modern, up-to-date, using state-of-the-art technology.
- Able to handle a bumpy road.
- Aggressive when necessary, but also knowing when to back off.
- You understand one another's idiosyncrasies, and know how to deal with them.
- Knows when to speed up, and when to take it slow.
- You can work on it, customize it, and make it your own.
- Simple to park and put away, but reliable and easily available at a moment's notice.

What is a midwife?

Like physicians, midwives provide prenatal care, manage and evaluate your labor, and deliver your baby. Many midwives are nurses who have been certified following highly specialized training and education (they are called certified nurse midwives). Those who didn't train as nurses, known as lay midwives, have a wide range of training and education, usually learning their craft by apprenticing with other lay midwives. Midwives are best suited to care for women with low-risk pregnancies. That's because they don't possess the skills to care for high-risk medical conditions or complicated pregnancies. Some women prefer being cared for by a midwife. Typically gentle and well-trained, they offer extra care and time with patients during labor and delivery. For this reason, many women opt for complete midwife care and rarely see a doctor. Most American women, however, continue to consult a doctor for their pregnancies.

Insider knowledge

If you are new to the community or just wish to do some extra sleuthing, call your local hospital's maternity ward or birthing center. Ask the labor and delivery nurses who they recommend as the top person to deliver your baby. These nurses work with the range of doctors and midwives every day, and can offer great insight to help you make your important decision.

What if I change my mind?

Sometimes, after establishing care with a doctor or midwife, women decide they aren't comfortable with their choice after all. If this is the case for you, evaluate the situation thoroughly, and seriously consider changing providers. Although it may seem a little awkward, it's best in the long run. After all, it's you who is going through pregnancy and birth. You owe it to yourself and your baby to make the experience the very best it can be.

Frequently asked questions

Use this checklist to remind you of all the important issues you need to investigate when choosing a doctor or midwife. A mental checklist can be useful to help you remember important issues during such a stressful time.

- What hospital or birthing center do you use?

- What type of birth can I have?

- What types of problems or risks might I be prone to?

- When do I get an ultrasound?

- Do you encourage childbirth education classes?

- How will you manage my labor?

- What happens if you are not available?

- Who covers for you and can I meet them?

- What can I have for pain relief?

- What is your C-section rate?

- Must I have an episiotomy?

- What happens if I go past my due date?

ShArInG tHe NeWs

News of the upcoming birth of your baby will be relished by family and friends, but when is the best time to tell them—and under what circumstances? Should you blurt out the information immediately for all to know? Or should you be more cautious and wait to see how the pregnancy goes before making an announcement to the world? Many women prefer to keep things quiet until the end of the first trimester because of the risk of miscarriage. Your personality type and situation will determine whether you shout the news from the rooftops or choose a more private disclosure. Whichever way you decide to share your exciting news, be sure you and your partner are comfortable with the decision.

Pros and cons . . .
. . . of shouting your news from the rooftops
✓ You receive loads of attention and gifts, and can share the excitement with others.

✓ You have a great excuse to exhibit odd behavior, such as vomiting in the street and demanding chocolate.

✓ You can benefit from other people's stories and advice.

✗ You might feel pregnant forever.

✗ The only thing anyone ever asks you is, "When are you due?"

✗ If you have a miscarriage or other problem, everyone knows.

. . . of hiding it until your jeans are bulging
✓ You and your partner have time to adjust and plan.

✓ If you miscarry or have other problems, you and your partner can deal with it privately.

✓ You won't have to suffer unsolicited comments from well-meaning friends and acquaintances.

✗ You may have to tell people you have the "flu" to disguise your need to lie down and interrupt your social life.

✗ You can't use the excuse of pregnancy to get out of having to do unpleasant tasks.

✗ Some people may be hurt or upset you didn't tell them sooner.

Telling tales
Once the news of your pregnancy has become widespread, prepare yourself for an onslaught of advice from friends, family, and co-workers. Everyone—even gay men and maiden aunts—has a pregnancy and childbirth story to share. Comments are usually offered in a spirit of love and concern, although you may not receive them in the same spirit. If stories make you feel worried, try to counter them with common sense, and share any worries with your doctor or midwife. They will almost always reassure you with comforting facts.

Quiz: hOw Do YoU fEeL aBoUt PrEgNaNcY?

Most women experience diverse reactions and emotions when they find out they are pregnant. Take this short quiz to see how your feelings stack up.

1. When the pregnancy test showed positive, what did you experience first?
a) Joy, glee, jubilation.
b) Worry, concern, upset.
c) Pleasure, but a little reluctance.

2. What are your major worries in this first trimester (12 weeks)?
a) I don't have any worries.
b) Financial concerns.
c) Threat of miscarriage or problems with the baby.

3. What does your partner/spouse think about the pregnancy?
a) It's the greatest thing that could happen.
b) It's a problem and a burden.
c) It's stressful, but we'll work it out.

4. When your family and close friends hear the big news, how will they react?
a) They will be happy for me.
b) They'll probably be upset or displeased.
c) They'll ask me how I feel and be supportive.

5. When you start to imagine bringing a child into the world, what are your feelings?

a) It will be lovely and wonderful.

b) It may not be such a great idea, but I'll do my best.

c) I have concerns about the crazy world I'm bringing a child into.

6. What financial concerns do you have about the new baby?

a) It's not an issue for me.

b) It's bothersome to me.

c) It's worrisome, but I'm working on a plan.

7. Do you feel reluctant to share the news of your pregnancy with others?

a) Not at all.

b) Yes, I'm stressed about it.

c) Somewhat; I want to make sure that I won't miscarry first.

8. What is your primary concern in your pregnancy?

a) To have a healthy baby.

b) That I don't experience major burdens in life.

c) To have a normal, healthy pregnancy without complications.

Your quiz results

Mostly As
You are extremely happy and incredibly well-adjusted to your new pregnancy. That's great! Keep in mind that it's also important to consider how the pregnancy will affect your daily life. Take some time out for planning, and think about how the new baby will influence your daily routine and those close to you.

Mostly Bs
You have a few important concerns about your pregnancy. That's OK. It's good that you are thinking matters through. Be sure to rely on family and friends during this stressful time, if you can. Also, share your worries with your doctor or midwife. You are a thoughtful and considerate person. Things are going to turn out just fine.

Mostly Cs
You are cautiously optimistic and put a lot of thought into your decisions. That's terrific! You'll feel better as you continue to educate yourself about what's happening to your newly pregnant body. It's great that you are reading this book. Continue to find answers to your concerns through books and reliable web sites, and by going to childbirth education classes.

Common reactions to pregnancy

In a recent medical research study, pregnant women were interviewed to assess their emotions on discovering they were pregnant. The most commonly reported feelings show how natural and normal it is to experience a diverse range of emotions all at the same time.

1. Elation

2. Pride

3. Shock

4. Fear

5. Worry

6. Guilt

ChApTeR 2

ThE gLoRiOuS ChAnGeS oF PrEgNaNcY

Not just in the Morning

Welcome to the first tell-tale sign of pregnancy. Morning sickness is a phenomenon even the least maternal of men have heard of, and most moms have experienced—about 75 percent of all pregnant women endure nausea and vomiting in early pregnancy. And it's extremely common to suffer day and night, not just in the morning. Why do they call it "morning sickness" when it can happen anytime? No one seems to know for sure, but pregnancy nausea may have derived its moniker because most pregnant women feel queasy when the stomach is completely empty, and that most likely occurs first thing in the morning.

What's the cause?

The primary culprit responsible for your unsettled stomach is the pregnancy hormone human chorionic gonadotrophin (HCG). From the moment of conception, levels of HCG in your bloodstream begin to rise—it's this hormone detected in blood or urine that triggers a positive response to a pregnancy test. The hormone continues to rise during early pregnancy and typically peaks around weeks 10 or 11, when nausea and queasiness are typically at their worst. After that, HCG levels begin to drop and other pregnancy hormones kick in. Fortunately, for the great majority of women, the queasy, seasick feeling halts by the end of the first trimester. In the meantime, some of the suggestions listed may help quell the nausea. If nothing else works, ask your doctor for a prescription for a safe antinausea medication.

top*ten*

. . . ways to ease morning sickness

1. Keep a few crackers by your bed and eat a couple before rising in the morning.

2. Eat what tastes good and worry less about what you should be eating.

3. Drink plenty of fluids so you remain well hydrated.

4. Consume clear fluids, such as frozen juice bars, gelatin, or water.

5. Try five or six small meals each day instead of the standard three.

6. Get lots of fresh, clean air and avoid smoke, strong fumes, and chemical odors.

7. Give yourself some chill-out time everyday: Take a nap, read a book, visit with a friend.

8. Take your prenatal vitamin with a small evening meal.

9. Ask your doctor about taking vitamin B6 and ginger.

10. Try acupressure wrist bands to prevent seasickness.

The good news

Yes; there is some good news about morning sickness. Doctors consider it to be a sign of a strong pregnancy. High levels of HCG hormone show your pregnancy is growing and thriving. So you might consider the associated nausea and gagging to be rather reassuring. That's not to say everyone with a healthy pregnancy will have morning sickness. Some lucky souls have a perfectly normal and healthy pregnancy and never break into a sweat or gag at all.

The other good news is that nausea does not affect the baby. During the first trimester, babies are so tiny that they don't have huge nutritional demands. So while it's important to do your best to eat as many nutritious foods as you can tolerate and take a prenatal vitamin supplement, your baby will still do fine if you can't yet consume a well-balanced diet. One of the most important things you *can* do is to drink plenty of fluids and stay well hydrated. And remember that even if you don't gain weight during the first trimester, the baby inside you is growing by leaps and bounds.

You can't keep *anything* down

If you haven't been able to keep anything down (including fluids) for 24 hours, call your doctor. Your healthcare provider will probably want to examine you, perform some tests, and most likely provide you with intravenous fluids. Usually this can be done as an outpatient, but in rare, more serious cases you could be hospitalized for a few days. Once the additional fluid is back in your system, you will feel much stronger and more able to cope.

topten

...foods to eat when feeling queasy

1. Saltine crackers	**6.** Gelati
2. Toast	**7.** Dry roasted nuts
3. Rice	**8.** Frozen juice bars
4. Bananas	**9.** Potatoes
5. Applesauce	**10.** Pretzels

ZaPpEd EnErGy

Fatigue is something you may experience from the very beginning of your pregnancy. Your energy levels feel zapped and, whatever situation you're in, you'd really prefer to be cuddled up with a big soft comforter and pillow, hibernating for a nice long while. Some pregnant women have an almost uncontrollable desire to sleep. That's just pregnancy hormones kicking in. These hormones are so important for the growing baby that they have a way of making you slow down and take better care of yourself. As the first trimester comes to an end, most pregnant women start to feel a little more peppy and find themselves zapping around again as normal.

Ways to feel better
- Do your best to eat well (see pages 52–57).

- Take your prenatal vitamins (see pages 58–59).

- Whenever you can, put your feet up and just rest.

- If you can, take a nap in the middle of the afternoon.

ThOsE bReAsTs— Va Va VoOm

Oh my! Breasts begin to swell and plump out almost the instant you get pregnant—which could be very exciting for your sex life, if it weren't for the accompanying tenderness. What's more, this new sensitivity leaves you yearning for a suit of armor to wear on public transportation during rush hour. In addition to changes in sensitivity and size, you may also notice differences in your nipples. The skin surrounding the nipple, called the areola, often grows larger and somewhat darker during pregnancy, and a few scattered bumps may appear, each usually smaller than a pea, protruding outward around your nipples. The technical name for them is Montgomery's tubercles. Not everyone gets them, but don't be alarmed if you notice them. They are completely normal and dissipate after the baby is born. Blame pregnancy hormones (again).

What's that stain on my shirt?

As pregnancy continues, some women find their nipples leak a little fluid: It might be colostrum (clear fluid thought of as pre-breast milk) or actual breast milk. This phenomenon usually occurs when your breasts are stimulated, such as during sex or a warm bath. Don't squeeze or further manipulate your breasts unless you want to spurt milk or even cause premature contractions. And do wear a supportive, well-fitting maternity bra. You might mention the leakage to your healthcare provider so she can make sure all is well.

Just Skin Deep

Most dermatologists know what to expect when they see a pregnant woman in their office. They understand how many changes occur in the skin during pregnancy, almost all of them completely normal and benign. You may notice new moles and age spots, and existing moles and freckles may become larger and darker. Some pregnant women become aware of a pigmentation discoloration on the face, especially around the eyes and nose, called chloasma, or the mask of pregnancy. A few unlucky women break out in acne, caused by various circulating—you got it—pregnancy hormones. If you are concerned by weird changes on your skin, it's best to see your doctor. She will most likely offer reassurance that everything is fine. Most doctors won't treat or biopsy skin problems during pregnancy unless they are very unusual or worrisome. Most changes and discoloration diminish in the months after delivery.

Fascinating fact
Most women experience a dramatic increase in breast size during pregnancy. Breasts typically gain two or three pounds by the end of pregnancy. So it's no wonder your pre-pregnancy bras no longer feel comfortable.

Tight stretch

Ranking supreme among the skin changes associated with pregnancy are the dreaded deep burgundy lines that run across some pregnant abdomens and thighs. Because stretch marks are determined largely by genetic make-up, there isn't much you can do to avoid them if they run in your family, although the amount of weight you gain plays a (small) role. The best advice is to be wary of creams and lotions that claim to prevent stretch marks. They hit your pocketbook and dash your hopes. Although it feels good to moisturize itchy, dry abdominal skin, this won't prevent the marks if you are genetically predisposed to get them (and olive oil works just as well).

The good news is that, with time, stretch marks fade to almost skin-tone. Plus, researchers are continuing to work on finding an effective treatment.

What's that line?

One morning during your pregnancy you'll wake to find that someone has drawn a dark line from your naval to your pubic area. Don't try to rub it off; it's caused by your pregnancy hormones, and it usually appears around the fourth or fifth month. The medical term for this skin discoloration is *linea nigra*, or black line. Contrary to an old wives' tale, it has absolutely no correlation with your baby's gender.

ExTrEmE pMs

If female hormones can turn a regular woman into a raging, tear-choked she-devil a few days before her menstrual period, what chance has a pregnant woman who's absolutely teeming with hormones? It stands to reason that just as your body goes through significant changes during pregnancy, so do your emotions. It's common to experience a mixture of feelings that range from euphoria to fear to sadness—all within a single minute. Once the initial shock and excitement of your pregnancy begin to wear off, life can become a bit of an emotional roller-coaster. The reality of pregnancy and bringing a new life into the world awakens all sorts of concerns and anxieties. Am I up to the challenge of being a good mother? What will happen to my relationship with my spouse? What about romance and a sex life? Will I be this size forever? What about my career? Will I turn into my mother—or his?

Hormonal stress

Understanding the effects of pregnancy on your frame of mind can help you manage your constantly shifting emotions. It's also reassuring to know that emotional stress does not seem to have a definite negative effect on the pregnancy's outcome. The growing baby inside you is very strong and resilient. Still, stress may have effects on you and your baby that medical science still does not completely understand. The medical community knows, for example, that stress can lead to a quickening heart rate or elevation in stress hormones. The fetus may feel these changes. Of greater concern is how you decide to deal with stress. Turning to unhealthy lifestyle choices, such as tobacco, alcohol, drugs, or junk food because you are upset will certainly not be in the best interests of your health, or your baby's. Instead try strategies that work to alleviate anxiety (see pages 38–39). And keep your pregnancy in perspective. Women have been having babies for thousands of years.

Pregnant thought

When you feel low, remember this: You are bright, aware of challenges, and already taking steps to make your pregnancy successful. The fact that you are reading and educating yourself about your changing body and mind says a lot about your future success. You have already taken a giant stride toward becoming a terrific new mother.

Ways to ease the stress

- Understand that your feelings are normal.
- Trust your emotions and have confidence in yourself.
- Keep talking to your spouse or partner.
- Get support from friends, family, healthcare provider, a support group, or Internet community.
- Don't try to be a superheroine; do your best, but always take care of yourself first.
- Educate yourself about what's happening to your body, and find out what to expect next.
- Participate in calming exercise, such as yoga and meditation.
- Release your inhibitions thorough energetic but safe exercise, like walking, swimming, and dancing.
- Listen to your favorite music or read an inspiring book.
- Splurge on a maternity massage.
- Take a bubble bath, light some candles, and place a soft pillow beneath your neck. **Note:** Unless your doctor has advised you otherwise, bubble baths are typically considered safe as long as your water has not broken.
- Learn relaxation techniques either through books or by booking a session with an expert.
- Keep a diary. It is a great way to express thoughts and concerns.
- Eat a well-balanced and nutritious diet (see pages 52–59).
- Give yourself an occasional treat, such as a few squares of high-quality chocolate or ice cream.
- If you can't shake off pregnancy blues, consider counseling to help you cope, or talk with your healthcare provider about anti-anxiety and anti-depression medication.

For men only

Pregnant women tend to be noticeably more hormonal and moody than their nonpregnant counterparts. The loving spouse or boyfriend needs to take extra care when communicating with his pregnant sweetheart. Here's a handy guide to appropriate responses to everyday situations. For more information on becoming a father, turn to pages 224–235.

Dangerous: What's for dinner?
Safer: Can I help you with dinner?
Safest: Where would you like to go for dinner?

Dangerous: What are you getting so worked up about?
Safer: Could we be overreacting here?
Safest: Here's 50 dollars; go enjoy yourself.

Dangerous: What did you *do* all day?
Safer: I hope you didn't overdo it today.
Safest: I've always loved you in that bathrobe.

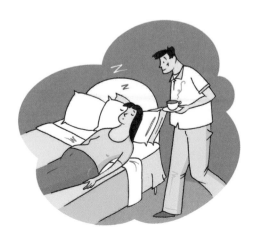

WoRrYiNg AbOuT mIsCaRrIaGe

No one wants to think about miscarriage, yet many women find it preys on the mind unduly during the early months of pregnancy. During these first uncertain weeks, many women are tuned-in to feelings of cramping or abdominal aches and pains, and constantly running to the bathroom to check for signs of spotting, bleeding, or unusual discharge. Usually there's no cause for concern. And, frustrating as it sounds, if there is a problem, virtually nothing can be done to prevent a miscarriage. Many people regard a miscarriage as nature's way of taking care of a pregnancy that, most likely, was not developing properly. Even so, miscarriage is a disappointing and sad event. Many women blame themselves or search for a reason for the miscarriage. In most cases, you won't find an answer. Studies show that work, exercise, sex, and most falls do not cause miscarriage. Likewise, conditions such as fright, stress, or morning sickness do not cause miscarriage. If the worst happens, it's important not to blame yourself—most miscarriages occur randomly and are not likely to recur with future pregnancies.

Mythbusting

The myth: Bleeding during early pregnancy means you are going to miscarry.

The truth: Bleeding is certainly something to have checked out by your doctor, but it does not necessarily mean you are miscarrying. In fact, the majority of women who experience spotting or light bleeding during the first trimester continue their pregnancies and deliver healthy babies.

You are bleeding or cramping

If you have any bleeding or abdominal cramping, be sure to see your physician right away. It could be a false alarm, but it's important to have a thorough evaluation by a medical professional. If you are not miscarrying, your doctor may want to monitor your pregnancy more closely. If you are miscarrying, your healthcare provider will want to examine you, perform various tests, and discuss treatment options. In either case, it's best to be under the care of a competent and compassionate physician.

Piling on the Pounds

Many of us have been so brainwashed by society's obsession with thinness, that we aren't quite rational when it comes to dealing with our own weight. When It comes to pregnancy, we are asked to step on that scale regularly. Both doctor and nurse need to track your weight progression and make comments about it as they go along. If you find this unnerving, don't worry. They aren't the diet police you may think they are: Try to keep in mind that they are doing this because the information may be helpful in monitoring your pregnancy.

How much weight should I put on?

It's good to have an understanding of what to expect as the pounds start to pile on. Most women gain only a few pounds during the first trimester, 10 or 15 pounds during the second trimester, and another 10 or 15 pounds during the third stage of pregnancy. Of course, this varies from woman to woman. The average pregnant woman gains about 30 pounds during a typical pregnancy. If a woman is underweight, she may be urged to gain a little extra. If she is overweight, she may be encouraged to gain a little less. Pregnancy is not the time to try low-calorie eating or the latest celebrity diet plan. It's paramount that you eat well-balanced meals. If you are healthy, your baby receives the nutrients that help him develop and flourish.

Where does all that weight go?

The distribution of weight for the average 30-pound weight-gain during pregnancy is detailed below. There really isn't much extra at all, is there? And most of the weight disappears with the birth of the baby, so don't stress!

Blood	3 pounds
Breasts	2 pounds
Uterus/womb	2 pounds
Baby	7.5 pounds
Placenta	1.5 pounds
Fat stores	7 pounds
Retained water	5 pounds

Fascinating fact
Weight gain in excess of 35 pounds during pregnancy may place you at higher risk of developing high blood pressure and gestational diabetes (see pages 95–96). Talk with your doctor if you are concerned about excessive weight gain.

Just an old wives' tale . . .

The belief is that if your husband puts on weight during your pregnancy, then you will be having a girl. If he doesn't put on a pound, then you're carrying a boy.

Let's Talk About Sex

Well, isn't that what got you into this situation in the first place? Sex during pregnancy is almost always fine and completely safe unless you have a high-risk pregnancy and your doctor has instructed you otherwise. Here we bust some common myths and misconceptions about sex during pregnancy.

Mythbusting

The myth: Sex may harm my baby.

The truth: Fortunately, with very few exceptions, sex during pregnancy is considered safe. Nature has provided excellent cushioning and protection for the fetus, making it almost impervious to harm. The baby floats in a bag of water held within the thick muscular uterus. The uterus is protected by strong layers of abdominal wall and the bony pelvis. Even via the vagina, the baby is protected by a closed cervix, a thick mucus plug, and a membranous, fluid-filled sac.

The myth: The baby will know we are "doing it."

The truth: A baby has no concept of sexual intercourse or genitalia. Chances are, the baby will sleep through your exertions anyway. The most any baby might feel is a gentle rocking motion, and mild pressure and movement. He won't have any memory of these events.

The myth: It's harmful to have an orgasm during pregnancy.

The truth: Orgasm is not harmful during pregnancy or at any other time. Having an orgasm will have no affect on the baby. In fact, orgasm may help relieve some of the tension and discomfort many women hold within their pelvic muscles.

There is, however, some truth to the concept that sexual intercourse can lead to contractions. So, if you are at high-risk for premature labor or threatened miscarriage, your physician may advise against sex until conditions have stabilized. In addition, women who are near term and want to induce labor sometimes find that sexual intercourse can cause labor contractions. In most cases, contractions won't happen unless your body is on the verge of starting labor on its own, anyway. However, sex may bring on contractions because semen possesses a certain chemical called prostaglandin that has been known to nudge things along. Ask your doctor how this might affect you. Doctors will also advise against sex if your bag of waters has ruptured, an important precaution to protect the baby and prevent infection.

The myth: Standing on your head after sex can increase your chances of becoming pregnant.

The truth: Although some medical experts agree that lying down after sex for 30 minutes can boost your chances of conception (because it keeps the sperm inside of you), standing on your head has NOT been proven to aid conception. In fact, you might hurt yourself trying to do it!

The comfort factor

You may find certain sexual positions aren't as comfortable in pregnancy as they were before; and this changes as your belly expands. In particular, you'll find yourself naturally avoiding positions in which your partner puts all his weight on your abdomen, which can exert a great deal of pressure on the uterus—a big discomfort as pregnancy grows. The up-side (literally) is that you'll have to explore to find new positions that are more comfortable—don't let me tell you which they are; have fun finding out.

I want it now!

You both may find that your desire for sex changes during pregnancy. Some women have increased sexual desire; others get more headaches. Either situation is absolutely normal. Certainly, watching your body change so visibly can be unnerving, and being racked with fatigue and nausea doesn't feel sexy. On the other hand, many women feel the need for increased affection and assurance that they are loved and attractive. Men experience change, too: Some are attracted to the softer and full-bodied pregnant form (that's code for can't get their hands off your gorgeous breasts). Others find sex and motherhood difficult to reconcile, and may even experience dark, Shakespearean guilt about their sexual desire. The best way through this is always to talk about your concerns. You may even grow closer sexually once you realize that intercourse doesn't have to begin or end in penetration. Sometimes cuddling and being close can be just as intimate. Relax and release your inhibitions and you might both find you enjoy these special months more.

WhAt A kIcK

There's not much more exciting in life than feeling your baby
move for the first time. Typically, you start to sense the baby's
movements when you are about 16 to 20 weeks along.
Sometimes it isn't completely recognizable at first. After all,
what do you have to compare it to? Many women say it feels
like a light fluttering—it's often described as butterflies in the
lower belly. But the sensation could be confused with having gas!
Often, by the time you start to think it could actually be fetal
movement, the fluttering has stopped. Don't be alarmed at the
beginning if the movement seems to come and go. Rest assured
that as the baby continues to grow, the sensation will happen
more often and become stronger. By the time you are 22 weeks
along, there will be no mistaking it. What an amazing feeling to
experience the little life moving around inside you.

Your inner soccer pro

Your family and friends probably won't be able to see or feel the baby
move through your abdomen for another month or so. By that time,
the baby will have started a regular exercise routine you can't mistake,
and people will be begging to rest their hands on your belly to feel the
baby. Every baby is different, and you'll soon become familiar with your
own baby's active times and sleep cycles. Why is it the baby always
rouses for a gym session when you're desperate to drift into sleep?

Tracking the movements

Some doctors require you to record your baby's fetal movements on a daily planner. Others just ask you to be sure to detect regular fetal movement. Once you enter your third trimester, you should be well aware of your baby's movement patterns. The important thing is to notice what's normal for your baby, so you can let your physician know if it alters. If you detect a significant change or become concerned, contact your physician for an evaluation.

ChApTeR 3

EaTiNg wElL AnD kEePiNg FiT

Eating for two?

You are the one responsible for supplying your baby with important nutrients, but scientific research has proven that you need to consume only an additional 300 calories per day during pregnancy. That translates roughly to an apple and a glass of milk.

Little and often

Many women feel much more satisfied and comfortable eating five or six small, frequent meals each day, rather than the traditional three meals. By consuming smaller meals more often, your blood sugar levels remain stable and your digestive system isn't taxed. It's also important to consume eight glasses of water every day. That keeps you well hydrated and improves your metabolism.

What should I eat?

Nutrients are substances in foods needed for good health, both for you and your growing baby. Examples include protein, fats, fiber, water, numerous vitamins, and minerals such as calcium and iron. Studies estimate that your body needs more than 40 nutrients each day, but how can you make sure you get all the nutrients you need? By consuming at least the minimum number of servings from five food groups (they're detailed on the chart) every day. No single food can supply all the nutrients you need. That's why it's so important to eat a variety of foods. Foods are the best source of nutrients because, unlike vitamin and mineral supplements, they provide nutrients in a natural balance.

The food groups: what you need every day

Food group	Daily servings	Sample serving
Bread, cereal, rice, pasta	9	I slice bread or ½ cup rice
Vegetables	4	I cup salad or ½ cup cooked vegetables
Fruits	3	I apple or banana, or ½ cup juice
Meat, poultry, fish, beans, eggs, nuts	3	2–3 ounces meat or poultry or I egg or approximately 20 nuts
Milk, yogurt, cheese	3	I cup milk or I ounce cheese

What if I ate junk yesterday?

Don't punish yourself or your baby if you are not as perfect as you would like to be every day. Just do your best to eat a fairly healthy and well-balanced diet, drink plenty of water, and take your prenatal vitamins. You'll thrive if you follow this regimen. If you have specialized needs or concerns, be sure to speak with your healthcare professional.

What not to eat

According to a warning issued by the Food and Drug Administration (FDA), pregnant women should avoid consuming farm-raised salmon, shark, swordfish, king mackerel, tuna, and tilefish. Although the chance of problems occurring is rare, it is possible that these fish could contain enough mercury to damage the brain of the developing fetus. Additionally, avoid raw or undercooked meats and fish, such as sushi, that could potentially contain harmful bacteria or parasites. In some cases, they could cause nausea, vomiting, and diarrhea. In more severe cases, organisms could harm the fetus. The FDA has also issued warnings against pregnant women eating Brie, feta, Camembert, and other soft cheeses. These cheeses are at risk for containing bacteria called listeria, which could potentially pose serious health risks for pregnant women.

Treat yourself

On a happier note, *one* piece of candy, sweet, or chocolate should be a daily dietary requirement. Of course, if you have diabetes or some other medical condition, this may not be a viable option. But if all is going well in your pregnancy, a special little treat every day may be just what the doctor ordered.

Vegetarian option

If you are a vegetarian, you can cautiously continue your diet during pregnancy. You'll need to plan your meals to ensure the proper nutrients for the baby. If you eat fish, milk, cheese, and eggs, it will be fairly easy to balance your nutrients. However, if you are on a strict vegan diet, you will need to make sure you consume enough protein. You may also need to take additional vitamins B12 and D to guarantee adequate nutrients for the baby. Be sure to discuss your vegetarian diet with your healthcare provider.

real life pregnancy

"Help; I can't tolerate milk."

"In my first pregnancy I got concerned that I wasn't getting enough calcium in my diet because I'm lactose intolerant. (I get bloating and indigestion after drinking milk or eating dairy products.) My doctor prescribed calcium supplements. He also explained that I could get calcium from some non-dairy foods, such as sardines, wild salmon, spinach, and fortified orange juice. That helped calm my concerns."

Annie, age 30

top*ten*

...pregnancy foods

A well-balanced diet chock full of nutrients, vitamins, and minerals is what's best for your baby. Here are some terrific healthy foods.

1. Meat, poultry, or fish: Why? Protein is the main building block for your baby's cells. Protein also helps the central nervous system develop.

2. Whole-grain breads: Carbohydrates provide energy for you and your baby.

3. Milk, cheese, and yogurt: Calcium helps build strong bones and teeth.

4. Lean red meat: Iron aids in the creation of red blood cells that deliver oxygen to your baby. It also helps prevent fatigue.

5. Carrots or yams: Vitamin A promotes good eyesight and bone growth.

6. Citrus fruits: Vitamin C aids the formation of healthy gums, teeth, and bones.

7. Pork and ham: Vitamin B6 helps the body metabolize protein, fat, and carbohydrates.

8. Fortified Cereals: Riboflavin (vitamin B2) maintains energy and promotes healthy skin. Vitamin E and folic acid help baby grow and develop properly.

9. Green, leafy vegetables: Folic acid is used to produce red blood cells and proteins.

10. Nuts: Moderate amounts of fat provide long-term energy for growth and development.

Don't Forget The Vitamins

In a perfect world, you would have started taking prenatal vitamins before becoming pregnant. Studies show that taking prenatal vitamins for a few months before conceiving can help prevent certain birth defects and give a better nutritional start for mother and baby. But things aren't often perfect, are they? So the best most of us can do is start taking prenatal vitamins as early in pregnancy as possible. A good prenatal vitamin gives you the added supplements your diet may not provide. All prenatal vitamins are essentially the same when it comes to nutritional content. It's just the flavor, size, coatings, and form (even coming in chewable or liquid types) that vary. Your doctor's office typically has different samples to try out. Experiment until you find the best for you.

A difficult pill to swallow

Many women find the first trimester an especially difficult time to swallow and digest a prenatal vitamin. Most of the pills are quite large, sometimes hard to swallow, and contain multiple vitamins and minerals that may be difficult to digest. That's especially true if you're suffering the queasiness and upset stomach associated with first trimester morning sickness. Use your common sense and just do your best. For example, you might be able to keep down a vitamin pill later in the day, in the evening, or after a meal when your stomach is full. Or you may find you can only tolerate a pill every other day or so. That's not ideal, but it's better than not taking any vitamins at all. If they all make you nauseous, speak with your healthcare provider about newer, more palatable prenatal vitamins that come in a chewable or liquid form.

Folate facts

All prenatal vitamins contain between 0.4 and 1.0 milligrams of folic acid. This vital nutrient has been shown to help prevent a birth defect called neural tube defect, especially when taken before conception or perhaps very early in the pregnancy. A neural tube defect is a rare abnormality that occurs when the baby's brain or spine doesn't close properly. Fortunately, neural tube defects are extremely uncommon. But you reduce your odds even more by taking a prenatal vitamin that contains folic acid.

Give me minerals

Your pregnancy and growing body demand extra iron and calcium. You may be able to obtain these important minerals through your diet, but if your doctor thinks you are deficient (he'll get a blood sample checked in a lab), he might prescribe additional iron and calcium supplements. In particular, iron can be quite constipating. If this becomes an issue, talk with your doctor about a safe stool softener or fiber laxative. Some newer and more expensive iron supplements have a stool-softener built right into the tablet. As for calcium, many doctors recommend Tums, Rolaids, or other such small chews commonly used for indigestion. They are considered safe during pregnancy and not only provide you with needed calcium but also treat pregnancy-related indigestion and heartburn.

ExErCiSe In PrIvAtE

Have you heard of the internal exercise routine known as Kegel exercises? Kegel exercises strengthen the muscles that form the pelvic floor. These muscles help support the pelvic organs and are important to tone the bladder, vagina, uterus, and rectum. When done properly and often, Kegel exercises strengthen the pelvic muscles as a good preparation for childbirth. They also can provide additional vaginal strength and tightness after childbirth. They may also help improve problems of urinary incontinence and pelvic relaxation that frequently occur as women age. And only *you* know you are doing them!

How to do them

1. To locate the proper muscle group for Kegel exercises, relax your legs and pelvic muscles. If you wish, try to insert your finger into your vagina and squeeze around it. If you feel your vagina tightening around your finger, you've located the proper muscles. If you prefer to try an alternate method, locate the muscles while urinating. During urination, squeeze your lower pelvic muscles and stop the flow of urine midstream. Do this only one or twice: Performing Kegel exercises regularly while peeing can play havoc with your urinary habits in the long run.

2. Now that you've located the proper muscle group, squeeze for about 5 seconds and then relax. Repeat for five-minute sessions, twice daily. With practice, you will notice the muscles becoming stronger.

WORK ThAt BoDy

It can be hard to muster the enthusiasm for exercise when you're assaulted by waves of nausea and fatigue, and your ever-increasing belly bursts out of your track pants. It's so much nicer just to snuggle up on the sofa with a soft pillow and relax. Although it's important to relax in this way, most days you should try to fit in some form of exercise, too. Why? Labor is a strenuous and challenging event that requires considerable stamina and strong leg muscles. I'm not talking about training for the Olympics here. But I do recommend a refreshing brisk walk or swim and some stretching and relaxing yoga poses. Exercise helps keep your muscles in shape and, more important to many pregnant women, it also helps you regain your figure more quickly after delivery.

Why should I exercise?

A sensible fitness program several times per week provides multiple benefits. In addition to preparing you for the physical demands of childbirth, exercise increases your blood circulation and thereby brings with it increased levels of both energy and relaxation. Exercise also provides relief from leg cramps, constipation, and backache. When exercising during pregnancy, it's important to not overdo it: You could overheat dangerously or wind up hurting muscles. Nobody wants that on top of the already demanding physical challenges of pregnancy. Follow the safety tips below and you can't go wrong.

When not to exercise

If you have health conditions, such as high blood pressure, preterm labor, or vaginal spotting or bleeding, your doctor may advise against exercise or place restrictions on your routine. Consult your healthcare practitioner before starting to work out.

Tips for exercising safely

- Always consult your doctor when deciding which exercise program would be safe and good for you.
- Avoid high-impact exercise and sports that involve sudden, jarring movements, such as strenuous aerobics classes and squash.
- Avoid sports that increase your chance of falling, such as skiing or rollerblading.
- Eat a high-carbohydrate snack about an hour before exercising to give you an energy boost (try cereal, a muffin, carrot, or apple).
- Put on a supportive bra to protect your sensitive breasts.
- Drink two glasses of water before exercising to provide hydration.
- Warm up with gentle stretching for at least five minutes before starting your routine.

- If you are not used to exercising, begin cautiously and slowly. Listen to your body and don't overdo it.

- Sip a bottle of water for good hydration as you work out.

- Check your pulse rate often if you know how. If it exceeds 150 beats per minute, take a break. If you don't know how, just make sure you can carry on a conversation as you work out.

- Stop exercising if you become extremely hot or dizzy; feel pain, headaches, or nausea; or suffer shortness of breath.

- Cool down with gentle stretching for at least five minutes after you've finished exercising.

- Drink two glasses of water after your regimen to maintain hydration.

Mythbusting

The myth: If you're out of shape, pregnancy is no time to begin an exercise program.

The truth: Of course, it's important to be sensible and have your doctor's blessing before you start working out. But in almost every case, even the most out-of-shape woman can begin a light exercise plan in pregnancy. Easy walking just a few times each week really can help you maintain your weight and prepare for the physical demands of childbirth.

Getting to know your medicine cabinet

It's best to avoid medication, whether pregnant or not. But when the flu strikes and you've got to keep going, some of us simply must take something. If this happens during your pregnancy, it's important that you see your healthcare provider for a complete evaluation and treatment. The doctor will take your health situation and the health of your baby into account when coming up with a treatment plan.

What's safe and what's not

It's always important to run things by your physician first. Even before any minor ache or pain occurs, it's a good idea to ask your doctor what medications are safe during pregnancy. Most doctors recommend you avoid all medication during the first trimester when the baby is forming important organ systems. However, during the second and third trimesters, when the baby is formed but still growing, most doctors will approve certain mild medication for their pregnant patients.

That Caffeine Buzz

Society is abuzz with caffeine. There seems to be a new coffee shop popping up on every street corner, and we're bombarded with advertisements for caffeinated soft drinks at bus stops and in store windows and magazines. What's a pregnant woman to do? Well, if you can resist them completely, more power to you. Water, milk, and fruit juice have many more redeeming qualities. But what about a little caffeine now and then? Medical research studies show that, in moderation, caffeine does not appear to harm pregnant women or their babies. Moderation translates to about 300 milligrams of a caffeinated beverage per day (see the chart to find out how much you can drink of what). During pregnancy, it's best to avoid caffeine altogether, but consuming it in low to moderate levels should have little or no influence on you or your unborn baby.

Drink	Amount	Caffeine level
Brewed coffee	8 ounces	100–300 mg
Instant coffee	8 ounces	50–190 mg
Espresso/ Cappuccino	2 ounces	40–70 mg
Decaffeinated coffee	8 ounces	1–8 mg
Brewed black tea	8 ounces	35–175 mg
Green tea	8 ounces	8–30 mg
Iced tea	12 ounces	65–75 mg
Soft drink	12 ounces	30–60 mg
Hot cocoa	8 ounces	3–30 mg
Chocolate milk	8 ounces	2–7 mg

Hungry for chalk?

Have you ever heard of pregnant women experiencing strange and bizarre cravings? And I'm not talking pickles with ice cream. Some pregnant women feel strong urges to eat nonfood items, such as clay, detergent, or corn starch. This is called pica, and it can be quite dangerous to your pregnancy. Talk with your doctor or midwife if you have these cravings. They can help suggest safer ways to fulfill your urges.

A tIpplE tOo FaR

Alcohol and pregnancy just don't go. Medical research studies conclude that alcohol can be damaging for you and especially devastating for your unborn baby. Alcohol causes your heart rate—and the heart rate of the baby—to drop. That may lead to reduced circulation to the baby, depriving him of important nutrients and oxygen through your bloodstream. It's also known that being exposed to alcohol in the womb can lead to various physical abnormalities, mental retardation, and, in extreme cases, fetal alcohol syndrome (FAS).

Just say no

Remember, when you drink alcohol, so does your unborn baby. No amount of alcohol is known to be safe during pregnancy, so the advice given to mothers in the United States is to avoid drinking any alcohol while pregnant—that goes for beer, wine, wine coolers, liquor, and mixed drinks. After your beautiful baby is born, by all means enjoy a special toast with champagne or the beverage of your choice. You'll relish it all the more.

What is FAS?

Fetal alcohol syndrome (FAS) is a form of mental retardation that also has characteristic physical deformities. It can also lead to behavior and learning problems once the baby is born. FAS is completely preventable if you don't drink alcohol while you are pregnant. Because it is unknown exactly how much alcohol causes fetal alcohol syndrome, the safest course is not to consume any alcohol at all during pregnancy.

NoT jUsT bLoWiNg SmOkE

We all know smoking kills. Yet, many women continue to do it. A recent survey showed that among high-school teenagers, girls smoke as much as, if not more than, boys. Now that you have the health of your precious baby to consider, you have the best incentive ever to quit—and to stay away from cigarettes after the baby is born. It's proven science that cigarette smoke gets through to the unborn baby. Smokers take in poisons such as nicotine and carbon monoxide through their lungs. These toxins get into the mother's bloodstream, travel through the placenta, and then directly enter the unborn baby's circulation. The poisons often constrict the blood vessels that supply vital nutrients to the baby, which prevents your unborn child from getting the food and oxygen she needs to grow and develop properly.

What's the risk?

A pregnant woman who smokes places her baby at increased risk for numerous health problems. Smoking can cause miscarriage, stillbirth, low birth weight, or sudden infant death syndrome (SIDS). A baby born to a smoking mother has a greater chance of being born small, underdeveloped, and sickly. The baby may also be delivered too early, before the lungs are ready, so she may have difficulty breathing. New studies show that the baby may be at risk if the pregnant woman's partner smokes. It's just not good for the baby to be around polluted air. Using tobacco in other forms, such as cigars, snuff, chewing tobacco, or pipe tobacco, also harms you and your unborn baby.

How to give up smoking

If you smoke, quitting can be one of the most important health steps you take to protect you and your baby. If you quit within the first few months of pregnancy, you can lower your baby's chances of being born too small and having many other health problems. Even if you don't quit until near the end, you can still help the baby receive more oxygen and get off to a healthier start. It's never too late to quit, but the earlier the better for mother and baby. Here's how:

1. Talk with your doctor or midwife about your desire to quit smoking. They can offer you literature and innovative solutions custom-tailored to suit your situation.

2. Do your best. If you slip up and go back to smoking, try to quit again. Failure only comes when you don't try at all.

When you can't quit

If you find you absolutely cannot quit, cut back as best you can. Cutting down is better than doing nothing. But if you cut down or switch to low-tar cigarettes, be careful not to inhale more deeply or take additional puffs to get the same amount of nicotine as before. Do try to quit entirely.

Fascinating fact

Decades ago, when a doctor wanted to stop a woman's premature labor, he would initiate a pure alcohol intravenous drip. The highly concentrated alcohol going into the mother's bloodstream would cause her entire body to relax and her contractions would usually stop. Needless to say, this method of stopping contractions is no longer acceptable. Thank heaven for modern medicine.

First Trimester Letter

To Mommy from Baby

Dear Mommy,

Hey, you there; yes you; hello, it's me, your little baby! I just wanted to say hello and let you know I'm doing great.

I'm still quite small, but I'm growing every day. Right now I'm about ten weeks old and about the size of a strawberry. You have done such a great job of making me a cozy place to live and grow. It's so soft and warm and comfy in here. No wonder I'm so relaxed and happy. I spend most of my time sleeping because growing requires lots of energy. Did you know I already have ten fingers and ten toes? I do spend some of my time moving around in here and kicking somewhat, but I'm too little for you to feel it yet. But just you wait; I'm going to be big and strong someday soon.

I was sorry to hear that you are feeling a bit under the weather. I hope you'll be feeling better soon. I'm so glad you're seeing your new doctor for regular check-ups. Sounds like you picked a good one. Hey, was that the two of you listening to my heartbeat the other day? Not bad for a little one, huh? I also wanted to say thanks very much for taking your prenatal vitamins. I know you don't care much for them, but they really do send me an extra jolt of energy. I need that added pop to continue to grow and develop. I really appreciate that you are trying to eat a well-balanced diet and live a healthy lifestyle. That shows how considerate and caring you are. You are going to be such a great mommy! I'm pretty sure I heard your voice the other day. It sounds nice. I love it when you talk or sing to me. Could you please do it some more?

Well, that's about all for now. Just wanted to let you know that I'm doing great. Please don't worry about me. I'm looking forward to seeing you, but not until I'm bigger and stronger. You seem so nice. I'm really lucky that you're going to be my mommy!

Hugs and kisses,

Your Little Love

CHAPTER 4
PrEnAtAl
TeStInG

GeTTInG tO kNoW yOu

On your very first prenatal visit, your healthcare provider will want to find out as much about you as possible. That includes lots of questions about your medical history, how you are feeling right now, and a complete and thorough physical examination. In addition, your doctor will want to check your blood for various important factors.

Blood tests and why you need them

Test for	Purpose
Hemoglobin and hematocrit	Checks for anemia; determines whether iron or other supplements are needed
Blood type and Rh factor	Establishes your blood type in case you need transfusion; also determines whether you need a Rhogam injection
Platelets	Establishes clotting factors within the blood
Immunity against rubella (German measles)	Checks rubella status; if not immune, avoid people with measles and get vaccinated after delivery
Syphilis	Checks for infection; may need antibiotics
Hepatitis	Checks for infection and need for treatment
Human immunodeficiency virus (HIV)	Determines status; may require medication

The pelvic exam

Also on your first prenatal visit, your healthcare provider will most likely perform a pelvic exam to assure all is normal with the pregnancy. The pelvic exam of the uterus and cervix helps the doctor determine the size of your uterus and ensure that your cervix is properly closed and not bleeding. During the pelvic examination, the doctor will carry out various laboratory tests to assess the status of your vagina and cervix. Like most of us, you probably don't relish the idea at any time, especially during pregnancy. Reassure yourself that barring complications such as bleeding, cramping, signs of infection, or high-risk conditions, this will most likely be the only pelvic exam you'll have to endure until you are just a few weeks from delivery.

Pelvic tests and why you need them

Vaginal/cervical test for	Purpose
Pap test	Gently scrapes the cervix to obtain a small cell sample; sent to laboratory to detect abnormal cells
Chlamydia	Checks for presence of infection; may need antibiotics
Gonorrhea	Checks for presence of infection; may need antibiotics

Hearing the Heartbeat

Hearing your baby's heart beat for the very first time ranks up there as one of life's most rewarding moments. And the thrill remains with you forever. Many women hope they will be able to hear their baby on their first prenatal visit. However, because this typically occurs at around week six to eight of pregnancy, it's usually too early to detect the pitter patter of the tiny heartbeat. Most women get to hear their baby's heart beating for the first time at around week 10 to 12 of pregnancy, or at the second prenatal visit.

What happens?

The doctor uses a special listening device called a doptone to hear the heartbeat. You are asked to recline on the examination table and arrange your clothing to expose the top part of your pubic area. The doctor places a conducting jelly on your skin just above the pubic area. It almost always feels chilly and wet. The doptone is a small hand-held device that uses ultrasound waves to listen to the fetal heartbeat. The baby is still quite small in early pregnancy, so it may take a minute or two to find the beat. But what an amazing marvel to hear your baby's first audible sound of life! It's important to differentiate your baby's heartbeat from your own. The baby's heart beats very rapidly, typically about 120 to 160 beats per minute. That's about twice the rate of your pulse. (Most women's pulse averages 70 to 80 beats per minute.) Be sure to ask your doctor or midwife if you need help distinguishing your baby's heartbeat from your own.

real life pregnancy

"Oh my gosh; that's amazing."

"I was about 11 weeks along and really hoping to hear baby's heartbeat at my doctor's visit. The doctor applied the gel and placed the doptone on my lower belly. All we could hear for about 30 seconds was static. The doctor carefully repositioned the doptone and angled it slightly toward the right. Suddenly there was a loud, rapid beat far too fast to be my pulse; it had to be the baby's heartbeat. The doctor smiled and I had tears of joy brimming in my eyes. It was amazing, and I decided then and there to bring along a tape recorder to my next visit."

Jill, age 28

Make a party of it

Once you've heard the heartbeat for yourself, be sure to invite your partner along to revel in what he helped make. Friends and family will also delight in being a part of the celebration. Invite special people to your next visit, so they can experience this wondrous feat, too. Lots of pregnant women bring along their own mothers. Things have really changed since grandma was pregnant, and she'll get tremendous joy from hearing her grandchild's beating heart. Some women bring along a tape recorder to document the baby's heartbeat. They play it for other friends and family to enjoy—and it makes a great keepsake for the baby album.

Doing it yourself

Many women try to hear their baby's heartbeat in the privacy of their own home, using either a stethoscope or perhaps a doptone that they have purchased. It's fine to do this, but there are a few things you should know. First, it's not possible to pick up the baby's heartbeat with a stethoscope before 20 weeks. The equipment is just not sensitive enough. Also, commercially available doptones vary from one to another. The sound you hear may differ from the sound you're used to hearing at your doctor's office. It may not be as loud and may be difficult to pick up. It might even sound more like swishing water than a tiny heart. It's almost always easier to pick up the heartbeat as the baby grows and the sound gradually becomes more pronounced. Try to be patient.

FaNcY nAmE fOr
A lIttlE tEst

Once you reach about 16 weeks of pregnancy, your healthcare provider will ask you to make an important decision. Do you want to take a blood test that checks for fetal abnormalities? The blood test is called alpha-fetoprotein (AFP). For maximum accuracy, this test must be performed between weeks 16 and 18 of pregnancy. To perform the test, the laboratory technician takes a small sample of blood from your arm. The baby is not harmed in any way.

What's it all about?

Medical research studies show that AFP can be used to determine various abnormalities within the fetus. For example, an elevated level may correlate to fetal neural tube defects. A neural tube defect is a lack of closure along the spine or brain of the fetus, and it often results in mental retardation. If the alpha-fetoprotein level is low, some studies have found an association with Down's syndrome, a chromosomal abnormality that results in physical and mental retardation.

How the test works

All growing fetuses produce a substance called alpha-fetoprotein. That protein is also found in the fluid that surrounds the baby and some of it crosses through the placenta into the mother's bloodstream. It's possible to measure the amount of alpha-fetoprotein produced by the baby by drawing your blood.

Analyzing your results

If your alpha-fetoprotein test comes back normal, you are reassured and no further testing is required. If, however, the level of AFP is either too high or too low, the doctor will pursue additional testing. The first test she will order is almost always a careful ultrasound examination, which will determine how far along you are in pregnancy. AFP test results could be abnormal merely because the pregnancy due date was incorrect. The ultrasound technician will also search meticulously for anything unusual and for signs of abnormalities. Depending on the results of the alpha-fetoprotein test and the ultrasound, your doctor may then recommend that you undergo an amniocentesis. This is a procedure to obtain a sample of amniotic fluid from around the baby. It is quite accurate in diagnosing problems, but it is invasive and has potential risks. There is more about amniocentesis on page 93.

The dilemma

Getting a normal test result is reassuring, but not a guarantee that all is well. Equally, abnormal results don't always mean something is wrong, just that more tests are recommended. This is where many women begin to stress out—and rightly so. If a woman is told her AFP test is not normal, she will become upset and worried until she has further tests that can reassure her. And that's the big problem with the alpha-fetoprotein test. It's not 100 percent accurate. It can only predict which pregnancies might have an increased risk for certain problems. In fact, most women with abnormal test results go on to deliver perfectly normal babies.

What should I do?

The decision to take the test is entirely up to you. It really comes down to what you would do with the test result information. If you would not have an abortion under any circumstances, then perhaps you should decline the test. On the other hand, if you want to have as much information as possible and keep all the options open, then you should go ahead and take the test.

Mythbusting

The myth: If the AFP test results show an increased risk for a genetic abnormality, you'd better prepare yourself for a baby with problems.

The truth: Most women with abnormal AFP results deliver perfectly normal babies. In fact, of the AFP results that show an increased risk of Down's syndrome, only about 2 percent of babies born actually have the genetic abnormality.

All aBoUt UlTrAsOuNd

Nothing brings home the reality of pregnancy like catching a glimpse of a tiny human being moving and kicking inside you. Depending on how far along you are, ultrasound allows you to watch your baby moving, kicking, or perhaps even sucking a thumb inside your belly. It's astonishing to see how content and happy a baby seems in the safety of his own little world—your womb. Most women have their first ultrasound around 18 to 20 weeks of pregnancy, an appointment almost always scheduled well in advance. Try to arrange to have your spouse or partner join you for the big event. It's such a big deal for most parents that some ultrasound offices even let you bring a blank video or CD to record live action shots for your home viewing pleasure. Be sure to ask ahead of time so you can be prepared.

How the test works

Ultrasound relies on high-frequency sound waves, made by applying an alternating current to an ultrasound transducer. The transducer is placed on your abdomen and sound waves are projected from the transducer through your abdomen and into your pelvis. Reflections of these sound waves are displayed on a monitor.

What is a level II ultrasound?

Sometimes your doctor will order a level II ultrasound to further examine your baby. This more targeted ultrasound provides an extremely detailed view of the baby and the baby's organ systems. Don't panic if your doctor orders this more comprehensive test. It's most likely just a precaution to assure that all is completely normal with the baby.

Why do ultrasound

The ultrasound test is noninvasive and has no known harmful effects for you or the baby. Indeed, it provides a wealth of information about your pregnancy to your doctor. This is what your healthcare provider wants to get out of an ultrasound exam:

- Identify the presence of two or more fetuses.
- Understand the position of the fetus.
- Measure the head, abdomen, and femur to determine the age and weight of the fetus.
- Identify fetal abnormalities.
- Note the location and maturity of the placenta.
- Measure the amount of amniotic fluid surrounding the fetus.
- Differentiate between miscarriage, ectopic pregnancy, and a normal, viable pregnancy.

Will I need more than one scan?

In addition to the standard ultrasound typically done between 18 and 20 weeks, your doctor may order additional ultrasounds if it becomes medically necessary. For example, if you have a high-risk pregnancy with twins or diabetes, if you experience bleeding or premature labor, or if the baby isn't growing as expected, you may need additional tests.

What happens?

You will be asked to have a full bladder for the test, so drink lots of fluids and don't use the bathroom. Some women experience mild discomfort from a full bladder, but it's necessary. Your bladder is located just in front of your uterus, and when it's full it causes the uterus to rise out of the pelvis for easier viewing. In a way, the bladder acts as a window and provides a much clearer picture of the uterus and fetus inside.

For the test itself, you recline on an examination table. The overhead lights are dimmed and a jellylike substance is applied to your belly. Then the transducer is placed on your abdomen and moved around. You will see the projected image of your baby on the televisionlike monitor. Don't be alarmed if you can't make out the anatomy right away. It takes years of training to be able to assess all the images. But you will be able to see the baby moving and the heart beating. Be sure to ask your ultrasound technician to point out various baby parts until you feel you have a good understanding and view of your baby.

Boy or girl?

Many couples want to know the sex of their baby. An ultrasound is often a good way to accomplish that task. The baby must cooperate, though, by getting into the right position, and must be old enough for the genitals to have developed. Most ultrasound technicians won't merely guess the sex. But if they obtain a clear image, they will share that information with you, if you want them to. Just be aware that the ultrasound is a test, and tests can sometimes be wrong.

Pros and cons of ultrasound

✓ You get to see your baby.

✓ It's not painful or harmful.

✓ You can check out the baby's anatomy to be reassured that everything is normal.

✓ You can often determine the baby's sex.

✓ You can see how the baby is positioned inside your womb.

✓ Seeing the baby on ultrasound provides increased bonding and connection with the baby.

✗ The image may not be as clear as you'd expected.

✗ The baby may look very strange to you.

✗ You may have trouble figuring out what you are looking at.

✗ You may not be able to determine the sex because of the baby's position.

✗ Your full bladder may be uncomfortable.

✗ You are usually only allowed one or two ultrasounds because of insurance and cost.

Sound of the Future?

Technology is ever-changing, and that includes ultrasound technology, where improvements are in development, such as the relatively new 3-D (three-dimensional) ultrasound available in some areas. This technology uses highly developed computer software to fill in the contours of soft tissues over the bony skeleton seen in regular ultrasound. The result is an almost picture-perfect image of your baby. The image can be so clear that many couples describe it as a photograph.

What's the catch?

There must be a catch, right? I mean, why would we continue to use traditional two-dimensional ultrasound when 3-D pictures are superior? Well, for one thing, 3-D ultrasounds are still considered experimental. Most 3-D ultrasound offices won't allow you near one of their machines until you've had a traditional ultrasound from your doctor's office. That's because, if there were a problem, they want your doctor to know about it first and to discuss the matter with you thoroughly. Also, 3-D ultrasounds are not considered medically diagnostic. That means they don't take measurements or check anatomy like a physician does during a traditional ultrasound examination. Instead, 3-D images are created primarily for entertainment and enjoyment. Some 3-D ultrasound offices even offer packages with different image options: color or black and white, stills shots or live action video, even shots set to your favorite tunes. Lastly, because it's not a medical necessity few insurance companies will shell out for a 3-D ultrasound.

That's not to say 3-D ultrasound doesn't offer valuable features. It's a joyful, reassuring experience to see such a lifelike vision of your beautiful baby. And in some parts of the world, a few high-risk specialists have begun to use the technology for improved diagnosis of birth defects. In such regions, 3-D ultrasound helps pinpoint the diagnosis and provides a useful tool when explaining problems to parents.

Pros and cons of 3–D ultrasound

✓ Provides a clear, lifelike portrait of a baby.

✓ Fun, joyful, and entertaining.

✓ Offers a variety of upgrades: photos, video, captions, music, and color.

✓ May be used in the future as a medical diagnostic tool.

✗ Costly, and not covered by most health insurance.

✗ Usually can't be performed unless you have a traditional ultrasound first.

✗ Does not provide measurements or anatomy checks.

✗ Baby's position may compromise the image.

How did that alien get in there?

Jennifer, a patient of mine, absolutely freaked when she caught the first glimpse of her baby on ultrasound. He looks like E.T.!" she exclaimed "Oh my God, E.T. phone home!" I suppressed my laughter and assured her that her baby looked perfectly normal. In fact, he looked absolutely beautiful. It's just that traditional (two-dimensional) ultrasound images show primarily bone and dense tissue. Seeing the baby's skeleton in this way worried her that she had an "alien" baby. After I explained that this is perfectly normal, she calmed down and enjoyed the rest of her ultrasound examination. She even took some photos home for her baby book. But she also mumbled something about signing up for a 3-D ultrasound next time.

Fascinating fact
When ultrasound technicians look at a baby's genitals on ultrasound, they either notice a "turtle" or "golden arches." That's true! A positive turtle sign is actually a view of the testicles and the penis (a round little turtle with its head sticking out) and indicates you're having a boy. The golden arches are the two female labia viewed between the legs; they indicate that you're having a girl.

GeNeTiC tEsTiNg

Occasionally, your healthcare provider will recommend a
specialized genetic test for the baby. It may be because you
are over 35 and so have a higher risk of delivering a baby
with a genetic abnormality, such as Down's syndrome. Perhaps
it's because a specific genetic disorder runs in your or your
partner's family. In any case, the decision to go through with
genetic testing is always yours. It's your physician's job to supply
you with all the necessary information, and to outline the risks
and benefits of the procedures. Then it's your call to make
a well-informed decision that best suits your situation. If you
decide to proceed with genetic testing, there are two
procedures to choose from: chorionic villus sampling (CVS)
or amniocentesis. Both are discussed in detail here. Don't be
alarmed if your healthcare provider refers you to a high-risk
specialist to perform these tests. That's a good thing. Having
the procedure done by an experienced, highly trained
genetic-testing professional reduces your chance of miscarriage
or post-procedural complications.

What is CVS?

Chorionic villus sampling, a genetic testing procedure that became popular in the 1990s, is typically performed at about 10 to 12 weeks of pregnancy, either in your doctor's office or the hospital. You position yourself on the examination table with your feet in stirrups, just as you do when you have a Pap test. An ultrasound examination is performed to determine the exact placement of the fetus and placenta. Then a small device is placed in your vagina, and the doctor uses a thin, straw-like instrument to suction out a small sample of placental tissue. Anesthesia is not required; indeed, most women don't find it painful. Many claim it's most similar to having a Pap test and pelvic exam. The tissue obtained from the placenta is sent to the lab for genetic evaluation. The results (typically available in one to two weeks) allow you to check on the genetic status and sex of the baby.

Pros and cons of CVS

✓ Performed much earlier in pregnancy than amniocentesis. This is a major advantage because you get results sooner and can make a decision to continue or end a pregnancy when you aren't as far along. Such decisions are always difficult, but many women prefer to have the information on which to base a decision as soon as possible.

✗ Does not screen for open neural tube birth defects as amniocentesis does. So if you elect to have CVS, you may want to have the alpha-fetoprotein blood test performed (using a small blood sample from your arm) at around 16 to 18 weeks (see pages 80–82).

✗ May be associated with a higher miscarriage rate than amniocentesis, although it's difficult to compare rates from the two procedures because CVS is performed significantly earlier in pregnancy, when more miscarriages occur naturally.

What is amniocentesis?

A tried and true procedure, amniocentesis is a genetic test that has been performed for several decades. It is the most common genetic testing procedure. Usually accomplished between about 14 and 17 weeks of pregnancy, the procedure may be performed in the doctor's office or the hospital. You recline on an examination table, much as you would for an ultrasound examination. Your lower abdomen is exposed and an ultrasound done to find the optimum place to perform the amniocentesis. Once a safe spot has been selected, the skin is cleaned with an antiseptic solution and then a long, slender needle is inserted through your abdomen. It reaches through the uterus and into the amniotic fluid-filled sac surrounding the fetus. Few women find the procedure painful, but many would say it is mildly uncomfortable, similar to a pinprick or needle jab. Anesthesia is not usually required. A small amount of amniotic fluid is withdrawn and sent to the lab for genetic evaluation. (Don't worry, the baby makes more fluid to replace what was removed.) The results (and the baby's sex) are usually available within one to two weeks. Unlike CVS, amniocentesis also screens for open neural tube defects.

Pros and cons of amniocentesis

✔ Has been performed for many years.

✔ Very few risks or complications when carried out by a well-trained specialist.

✘ Carried out later in the pregnancy than CVS, so you receive results considerably later (about a month) in the pregnancy. When time is of the essence in making the difficult decision to continue or end a pregnancy, a month's delay could be an important factor in decision-making.

real life pregnancy

"What's that between its legs?"

"I was very nervous about my upcoming amniocentesis. We'd already decided we wanted to know the baby's genetic status but didn't want to find out the sex. The procedure itself was surprisingly quick and easy. Afterward, the doctor was still looking at the baby on ultrasound. I asked, "What's that thing hanging between its legs? Is that the umbilical cord?" The doctor just smiled and said, "If that's what you want to tell yourself, go ahead." Oh my goodness! I suddenly realized what it was. I didn't think I wanted to know the sex, but I'm so happy I found out. The results turned out fine, and I went on to deliver my healthy, beautiful baby boy."

Susan, age 35

How about some sugar, baby?

During pregnancy, your body is at increased risk for developing a type of diabetes known as gestational diabetes. Rising levels of a certain pregnancy hormone can interfere with your body's normal metabolism of sugar and insulin. Typically, this occurs around the beginning of the third trimester. Fortunately, most pregnancies can handle these changes. But if the hormone overpowers the sugar and insulin metabolism, gestational diabetes can result. If you do have the condition, it's vital that you receive first-rate, meticulous prenatal care. The good news is that it almost always goes away immediately after you deliver. However, some studies show that women who develop gestational diabetes may be at a higher risk of developing adult-onset diabetes later.

Am I at risk?

Although certain risk factors make gestational diabetes more likely, you might develop the condition anyway. And because it's impossible to predict who may or may not get it, most healthcare providers test all their pregnant patients. The risk factors are:

- Obesity
- High blood pressure
- Being over the age of 35
- Strong family history of the condition

What happens?

The test for gestational diabetes is typically performed around 26 to 30 weeks of pregnancy. You will be asked to drink a sweet beverage supplied by your healthcare provider. The lab technician draws your blood one hour later. A normal result indicates that diabetes is unlikely and no more testing is required. A high level of sugar in the blood is abnormal and means you need additional blood tests.

If additional testing is required, you need to fast (nothing to eat or drink) for the twelve hours preceding the test). When you arrive at the lab, the technician draws your blood right away. Then you drink a larger volume of the same sweet beverage. After this, your blood will be drawn every hour, on the hour, for a total of three hours. Drawing blood at predetermined intervals gives your doctor an indication of how your body metabolizes sugar. If the blood test results are high, you may be diagnosed with gestational diabetes.

Getting a diagnosis

If you are diagnosed with the condition, your doctor will place you on a diet authorized by the American Diabetes Association. It's a sensible, well-balanced diet that limits candy, fruits, and other foods containing high amounts of sugar. Diet alone is usually enough to keep sugar levels within the acceptable range. However, if your sugar level is still too high, your doctor may start you on diabetic medication and teach you how to check your blood sugar level at home. He will also monitor your sugar levels closely. With good diet and monitoring, you and your baby should remain healthy. Occasionally complications do occur, but they are almost always the result of poorly controlled sugar levels.

Nothing to Stress About

Your doctor may recommend that you and your baby undergo a non-stress test. That's just a fancy name to describe fetal monitoring. The purpose of fetal monitoring is to ensure that your baby is healthy and tolerating life inside your uterus. The test may be ordered if you have high blood pressure or diabetes, are overdue, or have any other medical condition that requires the doctor to check on the status of the baby.

What happens?

The test can be performed in the doctor's office or the hospital. You recline on the examination table or bed, and a nurse stretches two wide elastic belts around your abdomen. To one belt, she attaches a fetal monitor to pick up the baby's heart rate. To the other belt, she attaches a monitoring device that detects uterine contractions. Every time you feel the baby move, you push a button, and a mark is made on the monitor paper indicating that you felt the baby's body. At the same time, the fetal heart rate monitor records the baby's continuous heart rate. Every few minutes or so, the nurse compares your record of fetal movements to the baby's heart rate. If all is well, she notes a correlation between fetal movement and a rise in the baby's heart rate, a reassuring sign that the baby is tolerating the uterine environment well. If the fetal monitoring is not reassuring, your doctor will discuss this with you and order additional tests, often a biophysical profile examination, to evaluate further the status of your unborn baby.

What is a biophysical profile?

This special test uses ultrasound and external fetal monitors to examine the baby's organ systems and determine her overall well being. It's often carried out when there is concern about the baby's health or if you pass your due date.

The five tests

The biophysical profile uses five criteria to examine and evaluate a baby's well being. Each of the five is assigned a score. A reassuring score means baby is doing well and thriving within the uterus. A non-reassuring score requires additional tests to assess the baby thoroughly. These are usually conducted in the hospital, in the unlikely even that immediate delivery is required.

1. Fetal breathing movements: The doctor watches chest movements using ultrasound.

2. Fetal body movements: observed with ultrasound.

3. Fetal tone: Leg and arm movements are assessed.

4. Amount of amniotic fluid: Pockets are measured via ultrasound.

5. Reactive heart rate: measured with external fetal monitors.

real life pregnancy

"That stress test was stressing me out."

"I was almost a week past my due date and pretty upset when my midwife ordered a biophysical profile. I was scared something might be wrong. She explained that the test was just to double-check on my overdue baby's well being and that everything was fine. Actually it was great to see the baby on ultrasound again, and the next day I went into labor and delivered a wonderful, chubby baby girl."

Libby, age 21

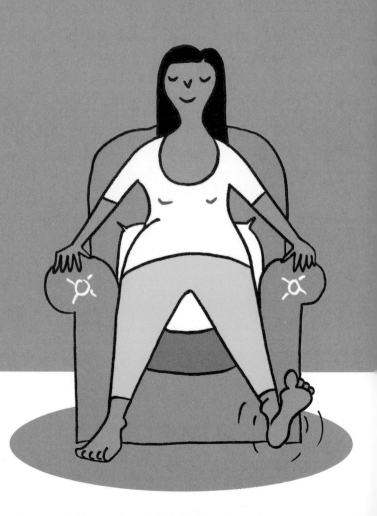

CHAPTER 5

PREGNANCY ACHES AND PAINS

TuMmY tRoUbLe

Most of us experience problems with the gastrointestinal tract
during pregnancy, and experience symptoms such as indigestion
and constipation. Although they can be debilitating, these
problems aren't usually harmful for your health or for your baby.
Rest assured, you will feel more like your old self again shortly
after the delivery of your baby.

What's the cause?

Increasing levels of pregnancy hormones cause the bowels to relax
so they don't function as efficiently as before pregnancy. Also, your
ever-expanding uterus is pushing and competing for space within
your pelvis, shoving your bowels toward your back and sides. It's no
wonder you suffer symptoms.

How to feel more comfortable

- Drink lots of water. It flushes out your system and helps keep
you regular.
- Increase your intake of fresh fruits and vegetables to boost natural
fiber in your diet.
- Eat six small meals a day. Smaller quantities aren't such a shock
to the system and keep your blood sugar level.
- Sit upright for two hours after eating a meal. Gravity helps keep
food moving in the right direction.
- Over-the-counter stool softeners and antacids are often helpful.

real life pregnancy

"I stuffed myself silly."

"Well, OK, actually this time it's my fault! When I was near the end of my pregnancy, my husband and I went to one of those steakhouses with an all-you-can-eat salad bar. We always loved those all-you-can-eat places. Everything tasted so great. I had my fill of soup, salad, bread, steak, and potatoes, and then topped it all off with ice cream. Afterward, we were walking through the parking lot and my husband said something funny. I started to laugh hysterically. My belly began moving up and down against my bulging uterus. Suddenly, I could feel my entire meal making its way upward. Eventually, I threw up everything, right there in the parking lot. I was so embarrassed. My funny husband suggested we go back inside and ask for a refund. The lesson learned? When pregnant, you just can't eat the portions you once did. It's best to satisfy your food cravings with small frequent meals rather than one huge feast."

Susan, age 27

Fascinating fact

During pregnancy, your bowels are moved around and displaced so much by your uterus that your appendix ends up just beneath your diaphragm instead of in its normal place deep within the pelvis.

Your Poor Aching Back

It's not just your baby growing bigger and stronger inside you; so are your uterus and placenta. All this means you're probably becoming more uncomfortable as your abdomen and pelvic area expand. This increased weight also places added pressure on your spine, leading to aches and pains in the lower back and backs of the legs, in the upper back, shoulders, and neck.

What's the cause?

Several factors are responsible for backache. First, various pregnancy hormones work to relax the muscles and ligaments in your back. So although your back is looser and more relaxed, it's also more prone to injury. Next, the weight of your ever-enlarging uterus, baby, and placenta becomes increasingly onerous to carry around. Both changes usually force a change in posture. With pregnancy, your center of gravity shifts and it's natural to alter your posture by throwing your shoulders back and pelvis forward. The resulting stance causes a waddle when you walk; sorry—that's just the way it is. All these factors do a real number on your poor, aching back muscles.

How to feel more comfortable

• Wear sensible shoes with good arch support.

• If you need to pick up something from the floor, use your leg muscles and don't bend from the waist.

• In general, you shouldn't lift more than about 15 pounds.

• Get out of bed or up from a chair slowly and deliberately, using your legs for balance and strength.

• Pregnancy yoga and slow, deep stretching can be very helpful.

• When sleeping, rest on your left or right side, not your back, and place lots of pillows in strategic places to form a comfortable nest. **Note:** The best sleep position during pregnancy is SOS—"sleep on side." It is somewhat better to sleep on the left side because it increases blood flow and nutrients to the baby. That's because the main vein of the body, the vena cava, runs down the back right side of the spine. There is no harm done and it is perfectly safe if you sleep on the right side. The important thing is to NOT sleep flat on your back or your tummy.

• Take time during the day to get off your feet and rest; it's best to recline whenever the opportunity arises.

• Indulge yourself with a fabulous, pampering maternity massage.

• Set a heating pad on the low setting and apply to the most painful area.

• Have someone apply an over-the-counter pain-relief ointment to your back.

• Be sure to check with your doctor about what's best for your situation.

Ugly Veins

Nobody wants varicose veins, those bluish, bulging lines that mark your legs and feet (and sometimes the pelvic region, too). Varicose veins are merely blood vessels engorged with blood. They aren't dangerous and won't harm you or the baby. But they are unattractive and do cause discomfort and aches in the lower extremities and pelvis. Although many women develop a few varicose veins during pregnancy, with some luck, they fade shortly after the baby is born and sometimes disappear completely.

What's the cause?

Your body produces more blood and fluid when you are pregnant. That means veins have more blood and fluid to drain than before. Pregnancy hormones cause the valves and muscle lining in the veins to relax. That means veins don't drain as well and aren't as efficient as before. So your veins have to work harder, even though they feel lax and sluggish. The increased weight and pressure of your uterus against your pelvis and lower body also contribute. The baby, placenta, and uterus act like a big road block that all the blood in your lower body have to bypass to reach your heart and lungs. It's an uphill battle. That's why you're more likely to develop varicose veins if you stand for prolonged periods. And, some women are just more prone to varicose veins because of a strong family history. If your mother or sister developed varicose veins during pregnancy, there is a higher chance you will, too.

How to feel more comfortable

● Get off your feet as much as possible. Sit down and put your feet up; better still, recline on either your left or right side, but not flat on your back.

● Whenever possible, place your feet higher than your heart.

● Wear maternity support stockings to give your legs some support.

● Wear sensible flat shoes with good arch support.

● Do NOT cross your legs; this reduces circulation.

● Massage your feet and legs with cooling, soothing lotions.

● If veins remain prominent some time after the birth, talk with your doctor. There are safe methods of removal when you are no longer pregnant, such as laser surgery or saline injection.

real life pregnancy

"But I have to stand all day at work."

"I work as a hairdresser at a busy salon. As my pregnancy progressed, I noticed varicose veins appearing on my legs. My doctor recommended maternity support stockings and told me to elevate my legs three times a day—and to use a bar stool at work instead of constantly standing. The varicose veins definitely got less prominent, and shortly after my baby was born they disappeared completely."

Kristen, age 36

Hemorrhoids

To put it bluntly, hemorrhoids are varicose veins in your rectal area—enlarged and swollen blood vessels encircling your rectum. Hemorrhoids are quite common during pregnancy; thus, it's good to understand them. Most women discover a hemorrhoid because it bleeds during a bowel movement. Hemorrhoids are also often quite itchy. Be sure to consult your doctor if you are having symptoms. The good news is that they are not dangerous and won't harm you or the baby. Also, they often lessen or go away completely a short time after the baby is born.

What's the cause?

Hemorrhoids occur from essentially the same factors that cause varicose veins (see pages 106–107). Because your body produces more blood and fluid when you are pregnant, the veins have more to drain than before. Pregnancy hormones make veins less efficient by causing the valves and muscle lining within the veins to relax. That means the veins don't drain as well and aren't as efficient as before. Then factor in the increased weight and pressure of your uterus against your pelvis and lower body blocking the easy flow of blood back to your heart and lungs. As with varicose veins, a strong family history of occurrence in pregnancy (a mother or sister who suffered with hemorrhoids) increases your own chances of having the condition.

How to feel more comfortable

- Don't sit or stand for long periods.
- Recline as often as possible on either your left or right side, and be sure to elevate your feet, legs, and hips.
- Sit on a donut pillow.
- Eat a well-balanced diet containing fiber, whole grains, fruits, and vegetables to regularize bowel movements.
- Drink lots of water to flush out your system.
- Enjoy a warm bath.
- Apply ice packs or cotton balls drenched with witch hazel for soothing relief.
- Over-the-counter medications such as Preparation H, Tucks, and Anusol are considered safe during pregnancy.
- Consider natural over-the-counter stool softeners.
- Talk with your physician to determine which course of action best suits your needs.
- If hemorrhoids are still prominent or causing problems after birth, talk with your doctor. Once you are no longer pregnant, they can be removed during a minor surgical procedure, if necessary.

Mythbusting
The myth: Every woman gets hemorrhoids during pregnancy.

The truth: Not everyone gets hemorrhoids during pregnancy, but some women are more likely to. Those who have a strong family history of hemorrhoids, work in jobs that require prolonged standing, or suffer from serious constipation are all more likely to acquire them.

LeG cRaMpS

If you've ever experienced a "charley horse," you'll know what I mean when I refer to leg cramps in pregnancy. I still remember awakening in pregnancy, sitting straight up in bed, and screaming as the searing pain seethed its way from the back of my aching lower leg to the spasm of my pointing big toe. Thank heavens, the pain only lasted a minute; it certainly seemed like longer. I remember wondering whether labor pain would be so intense (it is!) Even after the cramping stopped, my calf was sore for a day or two. Leg cramps are quite common during pregnancy, and though they are certainly uncomfortable, they aren't dangerous.

What's the cause?

There are a few theories. One thought is that your leg muscles are tired and fatigued from carrying around the extra weight associated with pregnancy. That's why leg cramps typically start during the second trimester and worsen as pregnancy progresses. Then there's the less than-optimum blood circulation your lower extremities receive during pregnancy, and the increasing weight and pressure of your pregnant uterus acting like a road block that forces all the blood in your lower extremities to bypass the enlarging uterus to reach your heart and lungs. There's another theory that leg cramps may be caused by not having a sufficient amount of minerals in your body, such as calcium, potassium, and magnesium. Studies have shown that deficiencies of each may lead to muscle cramping and spasm.

How to feel more comfortable.

- During a cramp, straighten your leg and gently flex your foot, toes pointed up and heel down. This stretches out the calf muscle.
- Do not point your toes downward; this can trigger a leg cramp.
- Massage your calf with long, gentle strokes toward your foot.
- Apply a heating pad on a low setting. This is soothing after a cramp.
- Avoid standing for long periods of time to prevent leg cramps.
- Never cross your legs; this leads to worsened circulation.
- Pregnancy-safe exercise, such as walking, may be helpful.
- Rotate your ankles clockwise and then counterclockwise for increased mobility and flexibility.
- Drink lots of fluids to prevent dehydration.
- Load your diet with plenty of calcium sources, such as milk, yogurt, cheese, and dark leafy vegetables.
- Eat a banana a day—a good source of natural potassium.
- Ask your doctor if you might benefit from taking a calcium/magnesium supplement at night.

Swelling

In case you haven't noticed, pregnancy brings about swelling in more places than your belly—like your legs, feet, and even your fingers. Some women don't seem to swell at all. Those are the ones that don't look pregnant from behind, but when they turn around seem to have stuffed a basketball up their shirts. (They are the same women who zip-up size 3 jeans to wear home from the hospital). Most of us have a different experience, since the majority of pregnant women swell up somewhat, especially in the lower extremities. Swelling by itself is not a worrisome sign, though it can be uncomfortable, especially when shoes and rings no longer fit. Some women buy larger shoes or open-toed sandals to give feet a bit of growing space. Many pregnant women wear their rings on a chain for the duration.

What's the cause?

When you are pregnant you have considerably more blood and fluid in your body. The ever-expanding uterus presses against some of the body's major blood vessels, making circulation much less efficient and bringing about swelling that's usually most noticeable in your arms, hands, feet, and legs.

Caution!

If you swell up suddenly, especially in your face and hands, be sure to call your doctor. There's a small chance that abrupt and extreme swelling may be associated with a potentially dangerous condition of pregnancy called preeclampsia. It may be a flase alarm, but your doctor will probably want to examine you, take your blood pressure, and run a few simple tests, just to be sure.

How to feel more comfortable

- Drink lots of water to flush out your system.
- Add lemon or cucumber to food. They act as natural diuretics.
- Eat fresh fruits and vegetables, and foods naturally low in salt.
- Avoid standing for long periods.
- Elevate your feet higher than your heart as often as you can.
- Recline on either your left or right side but never flat on your back.
- Participate in pregnancy-safe exercise, such as walking or swimming.
- Avoid fast food, junk food, and canned food.
- Talk with your healthcare provider about possible solutions to fit your situation.
- Don't take water pills or diuretics during pregnancy. They could be harmful to your baby.

When might it be a problem?

In rare cases, swelling could be associated with a potentially dangerous condition of pregnancy called preeclampsia (aka pretoxemia and pregnancy-induced hypertension). Preeclampsia is a form of high blood pressure associated with some pregnancies and can be potentially harmful to you and your baby. Besides swelling, symptoms usually include high blood pressure, headaches, blurry vision, and protein in your urine. Your healthcare provider checks for these symptoms at each prenatal visit. However, if you are concerned or notice changes between scheduled appointments, be sure to notify your healthcare provider at once.

Looking good

Every pregnant women wants to look good, and there's no reason not to. Especially as your pregnant body enlarges, make the effort to modify your wardrobe and buy or borrow some comfortable maternity clothing. Modern fashions ensure you stay looking smart and sexy, and offer figure-hugging options lightyears away from the kaftans of old (though even those are retro-stylish, too). Buy shoes a size larger (you don't have to tell anyone) if you need to. You'll feel so much more relaxed and self-confident.

StReTcH mArKs

It's really not fair: Our muscles and internal organs get pushed and pulled and shunted out of place in pregnancy as the abdomen stretches and reshapes and adjusts. If that discomfort weren't enough to contend with, the physical signs—pregnancy stretch marks—get etched on the skin for all to see. When they first appear, stretch marks are typically deep red grooves along the skin and may be red, irritated, and itchy. You most likely have your family to blame. In almost all cases, stretch marks are hereditary, so if your mother and sister acquired them during pregnancy, you probably will also. On the other hand, if your family is free from the deep red marks, then you may get off scot free. Fortunately, stretch marks do lessen over time, fading eventually to white or gray, and becoming less deeply entrenched than they once were.

What's the cause?

Although genetics play the major role in stretch marks, weight gain is an important factor. To put it bluntly, the more weight you gain, the more the skin is forced to stretch. If the skin has to stretch a large amount, a stretch mark may come along to mark the occasion. Even though oils and lotions won't stop the growth of stretch marks, they might provide you with some welcome relief. Stretching skin can become dry and irritated. So be good to yourself and indulge in a silky moisture-rich treatment for your ailing skin.

How to feel more comfortable

● Alleviate discomfort by calming inflamed skin with a rich moisturizer on the abdomen, buttocks, and thighs.

● Beware of the products on the market that claim to prevent or rid you of stretch marks. They only offer false hope and don't really work.

● If you're still concerned six months or a year after the birth, talk with your doctor about newer treatment options to reduce unsightly marks. Some doctors have prescribed combinations of vitamin A and C cream. Laser treatment is another option you could consider after you have delivered your baby.

SaFe TrAvElInG

Nothing beats a little R & R to improve your health and disposition. Taking a trip can provide much-needed relief from the physical and emotional demands of pregnancy. And who knows when you will get another chance to see a faraway place once your baby has arrived. The following information about travel during pregnancy may not apply if you are experiencing a high-risk or problem pregnancy. However, if you enjoying a normal and low-risk pregnancy, a little vacation or holiday can always do a body good. It's always a good idea to bring along your prenatal records showing your due date, ultrasound information, blood type, and any other pertinent medical information when traveling out of town, just in case a problem occurs and you need to attend a new clinic or hospital. It may save you from extra blood tests and other diagnostic exams.

Key concerns

The two primary dangers of travel during pregnancy are urinary tract infections and blood clots in the legs. Urinary tract infections are more common during pregnancy than before, and even more likely if you sit for long periods and don't take frequent bathroom breaks. Reduce your odds by standing up and going to the bathroom every couple of hours. That applies whether you're traveling by car, bus, train, or plane. As for blood clots in your legs, it's proven that pregnant women are more prone to develop them because pregnancy changes the coagulation factors in blood. The main danger is that a leg blood clot might dislodge and travel to the lungs, resulting in a deadly pulmonary embolus. Obviously you want to avoid that The simple solution is to get up and walk around. Stretch your legs, and exercise the muscles in your lower extremities to keep that blood moving around.

Car journeys

Always wear your seatbelt. Studies show that if a motor vehicle accident occurs, it's always safer for a pregnant mother to be wearing her belt. If you are involved in an accident, even a minor fender bender, it's always best to go to the nearest hospital and get a thorough evaluation. It might be overreacting, but it's better to be safe than sorry. During journeys, make a pit stop every couple of hours to visit the bathroom and stretch your legs. Also practice the exercises opposite. This helps time pass more quickly, too.

Air travel

Fly only in a commercial pressurized cabin. It may not be safe to travel in one of those tiny planes that allow you to roll the window down: They aren't properly pressurized. During the flight, drink plenty of water and take a walk down the aisle every hour or so, then practice the seated exercises detailed here. Many airlines require a note from your doctor that it is safe for you to fly once you are about 32 weeks or further along. Their concern is that you might deliver during the flight. One carrier in the southwestern United States offered free flights for life to any baby born on one of its planes!

Last-minute advice

Once you're within a month of your due date, most doctors recommend that you stop traveling and stay close to home, because this is the most likely time you will go into labor. Various pregnancy complications are also more likely to occur now. During this period, your doctor or midwife will want to see you more often, usually once or twice each week, to keep closer tabs on your pregnancy.

Easy travel exercises

Stow that tray table in its upright position and let's get busy! Every hour or so follow this quick and easy routine to keep your circulation moving in your lower legs and feet.

1. Heel lifts: Raise your heels up and down. Repeat 10 times.

2. Toe lifts: Raise your toes up and down. Repeat 10 times.

3. Ankle rotations: Rotate your ankles five times in one direction and then five times in the opposite direction.

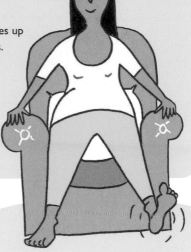

WhEn To pAnIc

Most pregnancies are healthy and happy. But it is still vitally important for you to be under the care of a well-trained doctor or midwife. In the unlikely event that you experience any of the following symptoms, be sure to call your healthcare provider without delay.

When to call your doctor or midwife

- You notice bleeding or fluid leaking from your vagina.
- You experience persistent headaches that are not relieved by rest.
- You suffer sharp abdominal pains.
- Your vision blurs, or you can see spots before your eyes.
- You experience sudden or persistent swelling of your extremities or face.
- Your temperature rises higher than 100.5°F, and you have chills, diarrhea, foul odor, or discharge.
- You experience burning or hesitancy during urination, or increased frequency.
- You feel uterine cramping or contractions.
- Your bag of water breaks.
- You suffer severe or continuous vomiting.
- You notice a decrease in fetal movement.

CHAPTER 6

GETTING READY FOR YOUR NEW BABY

GeTTInG eDuCaTeD

Don't be put off or intimidated by the idea of taking a childbirth class. These education classes are really wonderful! You'll have fun and acquire valuable information. Certainly, you won't be alone. Every pregnant woman in that classroom will be just as curious and concerned as you are about maternity matters. And as for the supporting husbands and partners, they know considerably less than you do. Childbirth classes can be very valuable to them as well. I can't over-stress the importance of you both learning as much as you can about your pregnancy and upcoming delivery. At the conclusion of your series of childbirth classes, you will probably receive a diploma. It makes a nice keepsake for the baby book. But the most important accomplishment is that you and your partner will understand what's happening inside your body and know what to expect as your pregnancy progresses.

What happens?

Most childbirth classes are taught by a specially trained maternity nurse. Classes are usually conducted in three to six separate sessions, lasting some three hours apiece. The majority of childbirth education is focused on teaching you what's going on inside your body right now, what will happen as the pregnancy progresses, and what to expect during your childbirth delivery experience. Having this understanding and knowledge is tremendously helpful to both you, as the expectant mother, and your spouse or partner. You'll find you are much more at ease with the entire maternity process once you are armed with the knowledge and wisdom to understand exactly what is happening to you and your unborn baby now and what will happen in the near future.

Pregnant thought

I've heard women say they aren't going to bother with a childbirth education class because they are planning to have an epidural for pain relief, or even undergo a scheduled and planned Cesarean-section delivery. My strong recommendation to them is that they should participate in the childbirth classes anyway. You may be surprised to discover that only a small portion of classroom time is spent explaining the options for pain relief and other methods of dealing with the pain of labor and childbirth. Most childbirth classes also teach incredibly useful ways to relax, focus, and breathe, and other coping techniques you might find useful outside the delivery room.

So you think you know your body?

Female anatomy is one of the most enlightening topics presented in a childbirth class. It's surprising how little most women know about their own anatomy. I suspect that can be blamed on society's hang-ups and the habit of referring to our female genitals as "down there." During childbirth class, you'll learn exactly what is "down there," how it works, and what purpose it serves. Don't worry; it's all done very tastefully and professionally. The nurses don't use live models and there's no blood or bodily fluids! Most anatomy is represented using plastic and cloth models. I still laugh when I think of the first time I saw a childbirth educator demonstrate the delivery process using just a plastic baby doll and a turtleneck sweater. She did a marvelous job. Some of the plastic models are more anatomically correct than that doll. And charts and videos make sure everyone has a better understanding of the female pelvis after completing the course.

What else is on the curriculum?

The childbirth educator spends a fair amount of time discussing the many aches and pains of pregnancy. She'll address backache, constipation, indigestion, urinary tract infections, leg cramps, and so much more. You'll get a reassuring sense of the regular changes pregnancy brings, as well as a better understanding of when to be alarmed and call the doctor. The teaching process itself is often livened up with videos, question and answer sessions, and small group discussions. There may be guest speakers, such as a general practitioner or OB/GYN physician, to offer additional thoughts and insights about the pregnancy and childbirth experience. An anesthesiologist may discuss labor-pain management options. A pediatrician might talk with the class about baby care, both in the hospital and at home.

Making friends

Most childbirth education programs encourage couples to share stories and talk among themselves. The childbirth educator encourages an environment of open discussion and lightheartedness by getting you all to play games, share stories, and enjoy refreshments together. After all, you are all in the same boat. Like you, other pregnant women and their partners have countless concerns and worries, and it can be comforting to meet other couples in the same situation.

In addition to the conventional childbirth classes, some hospitals and birthing centers offer specialized classes. Daddy Boot Camp is a popular choice among dads-to-be. If you are planning to breast-feed your baby, a breast-feeding class can certainly come in handy. You might also be interested in taking a newborn care seminar, in case you've forgotten how to diaper and burp a baby since your teenaged baby-sitting days. Some organizations also offer a class in infant CPR (cardiopulmonary resuscitation) for those wanting to learn this potentially life-saving technique.

Show and tell

At class, the childbirth educator sometimes provides a "show and tell" presentation. She brings in many of the devices and monitors you will eventually come across in the labor and delivery department. They might include fetal and contraction monitors, an intravenous (IV) line, a plastic device used to break water, an epidural line, and a vacuum suction cup or forceps to explain about deliveries that use such instruments. Some women and their partners really enjoy this hands-on experience. Still others shy away and don't care to see or experience any of it. It's your choice. The important thing is that you are aware of these things.

topten
. . . scary-looking pieces of equipment used in labor and delivery

You'll learn about these devices in your childbirth class.

1. Vacuum suction cups

2. Large metal forceps

3. Epidural needle

4. Suction tubing

5. Intravenous (IV) needle

6. C-section scalpel

7. Episiotomy scissors

8. Plastic hook to break your water

9. Fetal scalp electrode for internal fetal monitoring

10. Foley catheter for urine collection

. . . and relax

Yes, just as you see in the movies, at some point you will be asked to bring pillows to one of your class sessions. You and your partner will recline on the floor with your pillows comfortably placed around you. The childbirth instructor will dim the lights, turn on some relaxing music, and teach you several relaxation and breathing techniques. At the conclusion of the session, you may take a tour of the hospital or birthing center. It's always a good idea to know where you are going: Becoming more familiar with the surroundings keeps you relaxed when you make the transition from home to birthing place, and this can speed labor.

Pregnant thought

This interesting little conversation took place at a childbirth education class. The pregnant woman said, "My girlfriend told me that it's not really pain that I'll feel during labor, but instead it's more of a cramping pressure. Is that right?"

The childbirth educator smiled at her reassuringly and answered, "Well, yes, in the same way that a hurricane might be called an air current."

WrItInG a BiRtH pLaN

Many pregnant women and their partners feel it is important
to have a written birth plan. This document allows you and your
partner to write down exactly what you would like to have
happen (and often more important what you would like to
avoid) during labor and delivery. It expresses your wishes and
hopes for your ideal delivery. A written birth plan is not a
necessity. After all, the baby will be delivered whether or
not these hopes and preferences are written down or not.
Nonetheless, many women prefer to put their desires in
writing—it can empower you with a sense of control and
security at a time of great unease.

Staying flexible

Whether or not you have a written birth plan, it's vital that you
understand what is going on, keep an open mind, and remain flexible
about the entire birthing process. Keep the lines of communication
open at all times with your doctor or midwife. And remember, even
the best laid plans sometimes can go awry. Try to keep in mind that
every pregnancy is different and every birth is a special delivery in its
own right. There is categorically no right or wrong way to deliver a
baby. It's simply done in whatever way you can optimally manage.
Safety of the mother and the baby is always the first priority. If other
wishes and desires can be met as well, all the better. But keep in mind
that the most important goal is that we end up with a healthy mother
and a healthy baby.

What should I include?

Spend some time researching and considering the options at every stage of the birthing process by attending childbirth classes, reading pregnancy books and magazines, and connecting up with reliable Internet web sites. The more you know, the better informed and prepared you will be. Some of the things couples often specify in birth plans include:

- Preferred location of the delivery
- Amount of fetal monitoring desired
- Whether or not to induce labor
- Pain management required
- Under what circumstances an assisted instrumented delivery or C-section would be acceptable
- Number of visitors required in the birthing room for the delivery
- Plans to videotape or take still photographs of the birth
- Decision to breast-feed or bottle-feed

Pros and cons of writing a birth plan

Many medical professionals have some apprehension about written birth plans, feeling that they set up unrealistic goals and expectations and stop couples from staying open-minded during the birth.

✓ If all is going smoothly, it's fine not to waver from the plan.

✓ You talk and work with your doctor or midwife, aware that all deliveries are not the same and unexpected things happen.

✗ The plan becomes so important that you believe it must be followed to the letter and aren't flexible enough to change to do what's best for you and the baby at that moment.

✗ You might not be able to react if an unexpected problem or medical concern arises that isn't covered in your plan.

✗ If circumstances don't unfold as you'd hoped, you may become disappointed or upset, or you may even eventually suffer from postpartum depression.

The role of your healthcare provider

The relationship you establish with your doctor or midwife is enormously important in planning for delivery. It's absolutely paramount that you feel comfortable with your doctor or midwife, and over the eight or nine months of visits establish good communication and rapport. Be sure to discuss your expectations, wishes, and concerns with your doctor or midwife. Your healthcare provider wants a safe and wonderful birthing experience as much as you do.

MaNdY aNd mAtT's BiRtH pLaN

"We are submitting this birth plan to communicate our wishes regarding various birth-related issues. It is our goal to have as normal and peaceful experience as possible with minimum interventions. We understand that there may be unexpected complications or emergencies. In that event, we expect to be informed immediately and be presented with all our options, not just with standard hospital/physician procedure."

Inductions: NONE.

Early stage of labor: I will labor at home as long as I see fit and can manage.

Jacuzzi tub: We would like a room with a Jacuzzi tub for labor.

Pain-management: I would not like to be offered any medication during labor. I plan to do this in a completely drug-free state.

Vaginal exams during labor: To be kept to a minimum.

IVs: NONE.

Food: I will eat lightly if I am hungry.

Fetal monitoring: No internal monitoring; external monitoring to be minimized

Ultrasound: NONE, unless there is an emergency.

Positioning: I will be free to position myself however I like, including walking and squatting.

Breathing: No artificial breathing; I will use my own natural breathing patterns.

Amniotomy: No artificial rupture of the amniotic sac.

Episiotomy: NONE. I will use perineal massage and warm compresses for tear-prevention.

Forceps/Vacuum: NONE.

Cord cutting: Matt will cut the cord.

Delivery: Matt would like to catch and deliver the baby.

Separation: I want to hold my baby and immediately breast feed; the baby may not be taken away from me. Weighing and measuring can be done at a later time.

Washing off the vernix: Do not bathe our baby. We prefer that you rub the vernix into the skin as a moisturizing treatment.

Delivery of the placenta: I want to deliver the placenta naturally.

Hospital checkout: I want to leave the hospital as soon as possible after the birth.

Doctor's view

If all this works out, so much the better. It's great that the couple wants to be actively involved in the labor and delivery process of their baby. However, sometimes medical intervention is critical. For example, fetal monitoring may be necessary to assure the well being of the baby. Also, the partner may not be able to catch and deliver the baby safely. And the nurse may be unfamiliar with rubbing the baby's vernix (white cheesy substance covering the newborn baby) into its skin as a moisturizing treatment. This may not be possible to guarantee.

To DoulA oR nOt To DoulA?

Exactly what is a doula anyway? Doula is a word that comes from Greek and means "woman's servant" or "woman helping woman." In the world of pregnancy and childbirth, a doula refers to a professionally trained supportive companion who is not a friend or loved one but provides support during labor and delivery. Doulas are hired by you and are paid an agreed fee for their services. In years past, nurses often performed the role of both nurse and doula. That is, they were able to perform their medical and clinical duties but also be there at your bedside for continuous emotional and physical support. In today's medical world, that is often not the case. Nurses are generally overworked and care for a number of different patients. While they are still able to perform their required medical duties, they are not usually able to serve as a bedside companion, too. That's where the doula comes in.

What does a doula do?

Doulas are specially trained to provide you with information, emotional support, and physical comfort during your labor and delivery process. They are not trained nurses and do not provide medical or clinical care. Instead, they focus on helping you with breathing and relaxation methods, perform a gentle back or foot massage, and offer encouragement during your childbirth experience. Doulas charge a prearranged, agreed-upon fee for their services. Rates vary depending on the services provided and the length of time they are in your service. A general financial guideline is approximately $1,000, but this can vary greatly. This fee is not covered by any insurance plans.

Pros and cons of doulas

Some medical research studies have shown that having a doula attend your delivery has significant benefits. But partners may have reservations. It's vitally important that you have an open and honest discussion with each other before you decide to bring a doula into your birthing experience.

✔ A doula-supported delivery often leads to shorter labor time, fewer complications, less pain medication and epidurals, and reduced Cesarean section rate.

✔ Many women who use doulas claim to have a more satisfying birth experience.

✔ Both partners appreciate the added support and assistance.

✗ Partners and spouses may have mixed feelings about the presence of a doula, feeling she invades their privacy and takes away from their role as a coach.

Mythbusting

The myth: Having a doula at my side during labor assures me that I won't need a C-section delivery.

The truth: Although a doula can provide a great deal of emotional and physical support, she can't guarantee or promise a natural vaginal delivery. She can help you reason through what is happening to your body and why you may or may not need a C-section. If a decision is made that a C-section is the safest way to deliver your baby, the doula can still provide you with a great deal of assistance. In some cases, she may even be allowed into the operating room to support you during your operation. She can often follow the newborn baby into the nursery to assure you that all is going well with the infant. Or she can stay in the operating room until your C-section procedure is completed, then accompany you into your recovery room. Either way, she still provides ample emotional and physical support.

Stocking The nUrseRy

Here's a fabulous excuse for shopping—and you get to indulge your whim for cute stuff with frills and flounces (indulge all you can; by the time your little angel reaches 18 months, she'll be dictating what she wears!) With luck, you'll receive many of the baby's necessities during a baby shower. You may wish to register ahead of time for items you like. That way, friends and family members can select the exact items that suit your fancy. Never underestimate hand-me-downs from well-meaning friends and family. Baby supplies and equipment are very expensive, and kids use them for a ridiculously short period of time. So if you can borrow or receive second-hand equipment that is clean and in good condition, all the better for your bank account.

Baby's sleeping quarters

You will need to designate a special place for your baby to sleep. Many parents have the baby sleep in their room for the first months. After that, you'll most likely want the baby to have a space of her own. Lots of couples have a great deal of fun designing and decorating the baby's nursery. If you decide to paint the walls of the nursery, it's really best to have your partner do it instead of you. Better yet, hire a professional painter to carry out the job. The paint itself probably won't cause harm to you or your unborn baby, especially if the room is well-ventilated (if you're worried, choose eco-paints and avoid vinyl blinds, wallpaper, and carpeting). There's also a chance you could injure yourself or the baby by tripping or falling off a ladder. It's honestly not worth the risk. Besides, wouldn't you rather supervise than do the work yourself? Just tell the people what you'd like done for paint and décor, then sit back and supervise the job. Be sure to bring workers lemonade and cookies—and don't forget to compliment them on the fine job they're doing!

Necessities and luxuries

Choose pieces that securely hold the baby and provide some flexibility as she grows into the toddler years.

• What baby needs: crib and mattress, changing mat, high chair, sling, stroller, car seat.

• Luxury items: chest of drawers, nice closet, rocking chair, portable bassinet, changing station, baby bath.

top*ten*

...important stuff for your baby

1. Love	**6.** Crib and mattress
2. Car seat	**7.** Bath
3. Nursing supplies and/or bottles and formula	**8.** Baby diaper bag
	9. Baby seat/carrier
4. Diapers	**10.** Changing table
5. Clothing	

Pregnant thought

One of life's curiosities—why do they sell a baby's crib separately from the mattress? Seems silly, like buying a car and then having to buy the tires as an afterthought.

BaBy On ThE gO

You will need a baby car seat for your newborn. In fact, it's one of the most important purchases you'll make for your baby. Make sure you know how to install it before your baby is born. Most hospitals and birthing centers won't discharge the baby home unless the baby can be transported in a properly installed car seat. How do you choose from the huge selection of car seats available? Cost plays a part, as does your make of car. Check with your vehicle manufacturer before buying, since some seats are designed to fit better in certain cars than others. Some local fire and police departments offer free seminars on car-seat safety and proper installation. Check your local listings to see if this great service is available in your area.

Baby fashion week

You'll want to purchase or acquire the baby's layette well before your due date. *Layette* is a fancy term for diapers, t-shirts, socks, clothing, and various other accessories and toiletries for the baby. It also includes baby bottles and pacifiers if you choose to bottle-feed, and nipple supplies if you decide to breast-feed. Of course, you'll need some sort of portable diaper bag or mother's tote to carry all these things around with you.

Fascinating fact

Be especially cautious when placing your baby's car seat in a car that has passenger-side air bags. If the air bag goes off, it will strike the baby seat with considerable and dangerous force. It's safer to put your baby in the center rear of the car. If you feel that your baby needs to be constantly monitored or have extra attention, find an adult to sit with the baby in the rear of the car. Remember, no matter what type of automobile you drive, your baby's car seat ranks supreme as the most important seat in the vehicle.

Pregnant thought

Oopsie, baby! Babies don't care if they are wearing a hand-me-down outfit or expensive designer clothing. Your infant will spit up on whatever she wears. Babies seem to have a knack for messing up the most stylish outfits at the most inopportune times.

Choosing Your Baby's Doctor

Choosing your baby's first pediatrician is a big deal. Of course you'll want to feel assured that the pediatrician is competent and well-trained in the care of newborns. But it's also quite important that the pediatrician possesses a good bedside manner and a caring and compassionate disposition. That said, go for someone with whom you have a good rapport and can discuss issues in an open and honest way. Most women begin the search for the baby's doctor during their second trimester. This gives ample time to narrow down the field and get to know those who offer the most promise of a good match. Ask doctors you know for pediatrician recommendations. Your OB/GYN doctor and family practice doctor work with many of the pediatricians within your community. Hospitals and birth centers also have a list of referral doctors you might like to consider. Ask advice from coworkers, neighbors, friends, and family members, who might have useful information. And of course, you'll be checking your insurance provider listing to assure that the pediatricians you consider are covered by your plan.

Face to face

Once you've narrowed the field to several candidates, it's best to make an appointment to meet each one and conduct an interview. Most pediatricians will do a short visit for no charge. A face-to-face discussion is the best way to get a sense of what they are really like. Do they seem open, communicative, caring, and compassionate? Is the office clean, organized, and well-managed? Does it have a comfortable atmosphere? Selecting a doctor for your baby requires combining equal parts hard factual evidence and innate gut instinct. Arm yourself with the knowledge you need, ask the questions that are important to you, and be open to the feelings you experience when observing the pediatrician and office staff. Then you'll do a great job in picking the right pediatrician for your baby's first doctor.

Questions to ask your prospective pediatrician

- Are you board-certified?
- Where do you have hospital privileges?
- Does your office have separate entrances for sick and well children?
- Do you have a nurse who is available to answer phone calls during office hours?
- How easy is it to schedule an appointment with you?
- Do you have 24/7 emergency services?
- Who covers for you when you are not available?
- How do you feel about breast-feeding versus bottle-feeding?
- Do you recommend circumcision?
- What do you think about vaccinations?
- What is your child-rearing philosophy?

Mythbusting
The myth: After delivery, my doctor will care for both me and my newborn baby.

The truth: Of course, your doctor will continue to care for you. As an OB/GYN physician, your doctor specializes in the care of women. However, the baby needs its own doctor. A pediatrician is a doctor specially trained in the care of babies and children.

Second Trimester Letter

To Mommy from Baby

Dearest Mommy,

Greetings! It's me again. I just wanted to check in and let you know I'm doing great. Things are really going well for both of us now. I'm so happy, how about you?

I'm about 25 weeks old now and believe it or not, I weigh almost 2 pounds. I'm getting so big. Can you feel me kicking and moving all about now? I bet you can. Do you think that I should try out for the gymnastics team at the next Olympic games?

I've been spending lots of time listening to you lately. Your voice is so calm and sweet. I also really enjoy that fun music that you play. The other day, did I hear the Beatles? Mommy, you rock! Lately, I've also been hearing another voice besides yours. I think it belongs to Daddy. How cool! Tell him to talk to me some more. His voice sounds deep and strong; it's nice.

Oh, I've been meaning to ask you, what did you think when you saw me on the ultrasound? Did you get a picture of me? Gosh, I wish I had a picture of you. You seem so nice. I can't wait until I meet you—face to face.

Thanks for taking such good care of yourself. When you take good care of yourself, then you are also taking good care of me. For example, it's great the way you always buckle up your seat belt whenever we get in the car. I also really enjoy your many nutritious food choices. I especially loved that strawberry fruit smoothie we shared the other day. Yummy—let's have some more of those.

Well, I should go now. I still have lots of growing to do, so it's best for me to save my energy. I'll look forward to seeing you—the time is getting closer. Yeah!

Hugs and kisses,

Your Little Love

CHAPTER 7

HEADING
TO THE
HOSPITAL

WhEn To Go

You will probably know when it is time to head to the hospital for the birth of your baby. After nine long months of pregnancy, you've adjusted to your body and realize when something is changing or going on. You should also know what to expect as early labor begins because you've attended childbirth classes and done lots of reading and research on your own. Armed with all that knowledge and up-to-date information, you're in the best possible position when you hobble to the automobile to make one of the most important journeys of your life as a couple and as a family.

What to do

If you've been seeing your doctor or midwife every week during the last month of your pregnancy you will have had pelvic exams that tell you how dilated your cervix is and how the baby is positioned. Your healthcare provider will have provided you with instructions on when to call, when to go to the hospital, and what to do if labor begins after office hours. Nonetheless, here's a quick and easy guide to help with your important decision-making. Don't worry; be happy! Your baby is about to arrive.

Should I shower before going to the hospital?

It's certainly not necessary to shower before going to the hospital or birthing center. In fact, once you are settled in at the hospital, nurses often will recommend that you take a shower there. The purpose of the labor shower is not to become squeaky clean. Instead, many women find that standing under the water can be very peaceful and help them with their contraction discomfort. Sometimes spouses like to join their laboring partner in the shower. Please make sure that they bring along some swimming trunks!

Deciding when to go

Event	Recognizing it and what to do
True labor contractions	• Recognizing them: occur about every five minutes • Last about one minute each • Pain is such that you can't walk or talk through it • During a contraction, your abdomen becomes as hard as your forehead • Changing activity such as walking or showering does not cause contractions to stop or change their intensity • What to do: Regular and strong contractions for one to two hours should signal you to head to the hospital • If you are uncertain, go to the hospital anyway for an evaluation
Leaking amniotic fluid	• Recognizing it: Ask you doctor or midwife ahead of time if you should go to the hospital immediately or if you can wait a few hours • If not already present, contractions usually occur within a few hours of your water breaking • What to do: If your bag of water breaks, prepare to head to the hospital. You may want to call your doctor first.

	• If you've been told that you carry a specific bacteria called Group B strep, head directly to the hospital. Inform the hospital medical staff that you are Group B strep positive on arrival.
	• If the color of the fluid is brown or green, head directly to hospital
Bleeding	• Recognizing it: It's not unusual to have a scant amount of bleeding after a pelvic exam or sex
	• What to do: If you notice more than one spoonful of bright red blood, call your doctor and go to the hospital
	• If bleeding is accompanied by severe abdominal pain, go to the hospital
Lost mucus plug	• Recognizing it: You pass part of the thick mucus coating that develops over the cervix as protection during the pregnancy; it's a sign of the cervix ripening and beginning to dilate
	• You notice mucus discharge over several days or even weeks during the last weeks of pregnancy
	• Occasionally mucus is accompanied by a scant amount of blood
	• What to do: If you are more than 36 weeks along, do not be concerned
	• If you are less than 36 weeks along, call your doctor and prepare to head to the hospital for a check-up. This might signify preterm labor.

It's an emergency

Never drive yourself to the hospital. Always have a spouse, partner, family member, or friend take you. If you are completely alone, the safest way to get to the hospital is to call 911 or emergency paramedic assistance. This may seem like an extreme measure, but it's always best to err on the side of caution when the health of mother and baby are involved.

WHAT TO PACK

You may be surprised at how up-to-date your hospital or birthing center is. They are almost always well stocked and have essentially everything that you need to deliver your baby and keep you as comfortable as possible. Many hospitals and birthing centers compete among themselves to provide the best services and amenities. Fortunately, you are the beneficiary of the battle. Even though these places have many lovely things for you to enjoy, you will feel more comfortable if you bring some your personal belongings along. Here's what to pack for your big trip.

Showing soon

If you wish, you can ask someone to videotape your baby's birth. Just be sure to confirm that both your healthcare provider and the hospital or birthing center will allow it. Doctors and midwives often prefer video equipment to be set up at the head of your bed (which makes for more tasteful home movies, anyway). It also keeps video equipment away from the area where the doctor stands during delivery. However, if you do prefer filming from the below-the-waist viewpoint, that's usually permissible, too. Just ask your doctor or midwife where your camera operator can stand.

Some women designate a special friend or family member to be in charge of videotaping. If you don't want to do that, consider bringing along a tripod stand. The video camera can be set up on the stand, leaving your partner to focus entirely on you and your delivery, as it should be.

Checklist for your hospital bag

You may not need all these items. Check the list against things that are important to you and your partner. Those little extras make a birthing experience more comfortable, personable, and generally top notch.

- A couple of your own soft and cushy pillows
- Your favorite comfortable robe or housecoat
- Slippers or socks
- Familiar objects to soothe you, such as music, photographs, aromatherapy oils
- Your regular toiletries and grooming aids
- Long-distance calling card
- Phone numbers and address list of friends and family
- Camera for still shots, plus extra batteries
- Video camera and tripod, plus extra batteries
- Camera phone for instant photo messages
- Personal laptop computer
- Nursing night gown (if breast-feeding)
- Nursing bra and breast pads (if breast-feeding)
- Baby hat and socks or booties
- Receiving blankets
- Baby's special homecoming outfit
- Homecoming outfit for yourself (not your skinny jeans)
- And don't forget to install that infant car seat!

ThE bIg SqUeEzE

Just about everyone dreads the painful contractions of labor.
Reassure yourself that some amazing women don't find them all
that rough. And besides, in the end you get the most wonderful
baby in your arms. That's why some people refer to labor
contractions as pain with a purpose.

What happens?

A contraction occurs when your uterus flexes and tightens. By the
time of your delivery, your uterus is the largest muscle in your body.
So when that big uterine muscle contracts, you surely sit up and take
notice. Contractions of the uterus cause the cervix to dilate. The
cervix is the mouth, or opening, of the uterus. The cervix needs to
open in order for the baby to be delivered. So uterine contractions
cause the cervix to dilate; the fully open cervix connects to the vagina,
and that's how the baby will be delivered.

How will I know it's the real thing?

Many women are concerned that they won't be able to tell a true
contraction from a false contraction. That's perfectly normal. False
contractions are also sometimes called Braxton–Hicks contractions.
Braxton–Hicks contractions may occur for apparently no reason at
all and stop as suddenly as they started. However, sometimes
Braxton–Hicks contractions happen just before true labor
contractions. You may or may not experience these false contractions.
But rest assured that when true labor contractions occur, you will
almost assuredly know that it's the real deal. A simple, helpful chart
on the following pages compares Braxton–Hicks contractions with
true labor contractions to help you along. If you are still not quite sure
what you're feeling, call your doctor or midwife for clarification. Your
healthcare provider is very accustomed to these sorts of questions
and phone calls. Use the office number during office hours and the

after-hours number at night or on the weekend. Ultimately, the proof of true labor contractions is noting a change in your cervix. That can only be determined with a pelvic examination. So if there is any uncertainty at all, it's always best to be checked.

Comparing contractions

	Braxton–Hicks contractions	True labor contractions
Strength of contractions	• Fairly weak • Painless or not very painful • No change in intensity over time	• Strong and increasingly painful • Increase in strength and intensity over time
Timing of contractions	• Typically unpredictable and irregular • Stop as quickly as they begin • Non-rhythmical • Last 40 seconds or less	• Come at regular intervals • Continue to become closer together • Often occur every 4 to 7 minutes • Usually last about 1 minute each
Movement/activity change	• May stop or reduce in intensity if you walk, rest, or change position • Felt in the groin or lower abdomen	• Contractions do not stop, despite changes in activity and movement • Sensation felt in the back and radiates to the front of the uterus and into the pelvis

How to time contractions

The doctor will want to know how long your contractions are lasting and how far apart they are from one another.

1. To time the length of a contraction, simply begin timing when the contraction starts and stop when the contraction goes away.

2. To time how often contractions are occurring, check the time when the contraction first starts and count until the next contraction starts.

WhEn To InDuCe LaBoR

Induction of labor means the doctor or midwife performs a procedure or provides medication that causes your body to go into labor before it would naturally. In the United States, about 15 percent of all pregnant women have their labor induced. Medical inductions are usually pretty straightforward, very low-risk, and usually not very controversial. If you have a medical illness or condition that affects your pregnancy, you are probably already fully aware of it. The doctor has most likely been monitoring you and the baby throughout your pregnancy, and the doctor's suggestion to induce labor probably comes as no surprise. That should also be the case if your water breaks and you don't spontaneously start contracting, or you go way past your due date. The more controversial reason for induction is purely elective, providing convenience to the healthcare provider, the patient, or both.

Why would I be induced?

Your healthcare provider may discuss labor induction because of a medical reason. This might happen if you have a health condition or complication that causes difficulties with your pregnancy, either for you or the baby, and makes it important to deliver the baby sooner to avoid further medical problems. When the water breaks, in most cases, your body spontaneously starts having contractions. However, if, unusually, you do not, your doctor or midwife will suggest augmenting your labor by inducing contractions. Once your water has broken, it's best to deliver the baby within 24 hours to avoid the risk of infection.

Reasons for medically indicated labor induction

- Gestational diabetes
- High blood pressure or pre-eclampsia
- An infection within the uterus
- Problems with the placenta
- Internal bleeding
- Lupus
- Heart condition
- A known medical problem with the baby
- Your water has broken but you are not having contractions

real life pregnancy

"Hup, two, three, four . . ."

"I'm an accountant in the U.S. Army and extremely number oriented. My first child's due date was March 3, 2001, but I'd convinced myself how great it would be to have the baby born on March 2. That way, the baby's birthday would be 03-02-01, just like a countdown. As it turned out, the hospital was too busy to accommodate my elective induction date and I ended up delivering the baby spontaneously on March 4. I was actually very happy with his birthday because March 4 sounds just like that familiar military command, "March forth!"

Kathleen, age 30

Why choose induction?

Elective induction of labor is a controversial subject. In this case, contractions are brought about because the doctor or patient, or both, would like to have the baby delivered sooner than nature planned. This may be because the doctor is on vacation at the due date. Or perhaps you'd like to select a special date for your baby's birthday. (Induction is not a precise science and may not guarantee your delivery on an exact day.) Naturally, extreme caution must be used before agreeing to undergo such an elective and otherwise unnecessary procedure. The primary concern is that your baby is mature enough and ready to be delivered. The last thing you want is for a baby to be delivered prematurely or with health problems. That's why most healthcare providers will not allow elective inductions unless the baby is within a week or so of the due date. Even then, the procedure is somewhat controversial because it relies on a due date that may or may not be accurate. For additional assurance, some doctors order an ultrasound before elective induction to estimate the baby's size and weight. On occasion, the doctor might even perform an amniocentesis to check the baby's amniotic fluid. A special test can be run on the baby's amniotic fluid in just a few hours to determine whether or not the baby's lungs are mature and ready to breathe in a regular air environment.

Questions to ask about labor induction

It's always best to talk openly and honestly about any concerns to your doctor. Don't be embarrassed or intimidated. Here are some important questions to ask.

- Why am I being induced?
- What would happen if I don't agree to be induced?
- What are the risks and benefits of being induced?
- What are risks and benefits to the baby of being induced?
- How long will the induction take?
- How do you plan to induce me?
- Is it possible that the induction won't work? Then what?
- Does induction raise my chances of having a C-section?
- Are there any other special considerations for my particular situation?

Seek patience

Being overdue can be a frustrating and uncomfortable situation. Knowing what's going on in your body and understanding your options, however, can put your mind at ease. Clearly, there are many ways for delivery to be induced, and if needed, your doctor will find the right one for you. Just try to keep in mind the good news: The majority of babies that arrive after their estimated due dates are born healthy and develop normally.

Ways To Be InDuCeD

Once the decision has been made to induce you, it's important for you to understand the various methods that might be used for the procedure. Depending on how dilated your cervix is, a number of techniques are used to induce contractions. For example, if your cervix has already dilated by two to three centimeters and is at least 50 percent effaced (thinned out), induction will likely be an easy process. But, if your cervix is closed and thick, several methods may be required over a period of days in order to prepare it for labor. Work with your healthcare provider to determine which method best suits you.

Mechanical device (Foley bulb or laminaria)

The Foley bulb is a small balloon-like device that is inserted into your cervix while deflated, and then inflated to about 1 centimeter. It's usually kept in your cervix for several hours or until it falls out. The laminaria is similar, but it resembles a small, thin twig made of seaweed. Several laminaria are soaked in water and placed in your cervix. Over a few hours they expand and slowly dilate your cervix to about 1 centimeter. They typically stay in a few hours or until they fall out. Both methods feel similar to a pelvic exam and are used to soften and ripen the cervix when it is not yet ready to dilate or efface easily on its own. Neither procedure poses a risk to the baby, and both are almost always performed in the doctor's office.

Stripping membranes

Part of a pelvic exam, this technique is used to stretch and stimulate a cervix that is already somewhat dilated and seems ready to further dilate and efface easily on its own. The procedure is almost always done in the doctor's office. During a pelvic exam, your doctor or midwife sweeps a finger over the membranes to separate them slightly from the cervix. There is no danger to the baby.

Breaking bag of water (membranes)

This procedure is always performed in the hospital for safety reasons (it requires fetal monitoring). During a pelvic exam, the doctor uses a small plastic hook to rupture the membranes artificially. It's usually done when the cervix seems ripe and ready to deliver. The act of rupturing the membranes usually causes the uterus to contract. Once the bag of water is broken, the general guideline is to deliver the baby within twenty-four hours to reduce the chance of infection.

Intravenous (IV) pitocin

Pitocin is a special medication that causes the uterus to contract. It is often given when the bag of water is broken artificially and is typically used when the cervix is ripe and ready for labor. This medication is always given in hospital for safety because it requires fetal monitoring.

Prostaglandin by mouth or vagina

Prostaglandin tablets may be used either when the cervix seems ready for labor, or given as a way of softening the cervix when it is still thick and firm. Tablets are taken orally, or suppositories are placed within the vagina. This is always done in the hospital for safety because it requires fetal monitoring.

Is induction risky?

If your cervix is ready for labor, there is very little risk associated with labor induction. Very rarely will fetal distress or uterine rupture occur as a result of the induction. In the very unlikely event of an emergency, an urgent C-section might be required.

Mythbusting

The myth: Having labor induced hurts more than having labor start on its own.

The Truth: When you're induced, you are admitted to the hospital when you are not in labor, so you aren't experiencing any pain at all. Within a few hours of labor induction, contractions begin and, of course, that results in pain. Some women remember how, just a few hours earlier, they felt fine, and they feel the contraction pain in jolting contrast to their earlier comfort. However, once contractions develop into a regular rhythm, pain is at the same level of intensity whether it was induced artificially or came about spontaneously.

CHAPTER 8

YOUR SPECIAL DELIVERY

Arriving At The Hospital

When you first get to the hospital, a nurse will greet you and probably move you into a triage unit. That's a special area of the labor and delivery department where your condition can be assessed. You will first have a brief interview to determine what brought you to the hospital and allow you to express any concerns. Because your doctor's office will have previously sent your medical file to the hospital, the nurse will be able to access your prenatal records and have your pregnancy and medical history available.

What checks will they do?

Your blood pressure and other vital signs will be checked, often in the triage area, and the nurse will strap two wide elastic belts around your waist. One belt has a monitor to check for the baby's heart rate. The other belt has a monitor that evaluates your uterine contractions. The nurse will perform a pelvic exam to determine the status of your cervix. She'll check to see how dilated and effaced (thinned out) your cervix is, and also determine the position of the baby's head within your pelvis. Once your evaluation is complete, the nurse will call your doctor or midwife to update them on your status. Your healthcare provider will use that information to determine whether to admit you to the labor and delivery ward or to send you home. If you are admitted, you will most likely be transferred to a birthing room.

top*ten*

... people you'll meet at the hospital

1. Receptionist	**6.** Nursery nurse
2. Triage nurse	**7.** Pediatrician
3. Labor and delivery nurse	**8.** Postpartum nurse
4. OB/GYN doctor	**9.** Lactation consultant
5. Anesthesiologist	**10.** Food service workers

real life pregnancy

"I was terrified."

"I was so nervous when I got to the hospital in labor. I couldn't take my eyes off the monitors for fear the baby would have fetal distress and nobody would know about it. The nurse explained that the monitors come with alarms that beep and flash when the baby might be distressed, which made me feel a little better. She also told me about the central monitoring system at the nurse's stations—the entire medical team could monitor my baby's safety without me even knowing. When I found out I was in such a safe environment, I finally relaxed."

Connie, age 41

Aʟʟ aʙᴏᴜt Mᴏɴɪtᴏʀɪɴɢ

Mothers in the United States usually have a considerable amount of fetal monitoring during labor. As you settle into your hospital birthing room, you'll most likely be attached to a fetal monitor again. It's important for the medical team to track the baby's heart rate during labor. Uterine contractions can be stressful to the baby as the uterine muscle squeezes and contracts. Fetal monitoring tells your doctor and nurses that your baby is doing all right during these contractions. Your healthcare provider will also monitor your contractions, so she can compare your contraction pattern to the baby's heart rate pattern. Certain patterns are known to be reassuring and indicate fetal well being. Other patterns are more concerning and may indicate fetal distress. Your healthcare provider and nurse will watch both the fetal heart tracing and the contraction monitoring very closely.

European mothers

In Europe and other parts of the world where midwives play a major role in the birthing process, labor and birth involve less fetal monitoring. Home births and birthing center deliveries are much more common. In these circumstances, the baby is often monitored only every 15 minutes with a hand-held Doppler device.

Turn down the volume!

I entered one labor room where the fetal heart tone monitor was so loud that the birth couple could hardly carry on a conversation. I asked them why it was so loud. They said that it had been that way since they arrived, four hours earlier. With one turn of a dial, I switched the volume to a more tolerable tone. They were so relieved. "We had no idea that the monitor had a volume button; we just thought we had a loud baby."

real life pregnancy

How do fetal monitors work?

Most of the time, fetal monitoring is performed externally. That means the wide elastic belt around your waist is attached to a small, round monitoring device that transmits the baby's heartbeat. In some situations, external monitoring isn't sufficient. For example, if the baby is lying in a position in which it's difficult to pick up the heartrate or if there is meconium (baby stool) stained fluid, closer monitoring may be required. That's when internal fetal monitoring is used. For internal fetal monitoring a small wire is attached to your baby's scalp. This does not harm your baby. Your membranes must be ruptured and your cervix dilated at least 1 centimeter in order for an internal monitor to work properly. Fetal monitoring may be either intermittent or continuous.

That decision is usually left to your healthcare provider and depends on whether you have a high- or low-risk pregnancy and how the baby seems to be tolerating labor contractions.

Monitoring contractions

Similar to fetal monitoring, contraction monitoring can be done externally or internally. Most women are monitored externally by a wide, elastic belt placed around the belly with a small, round monitor attached to it that picks up the presence of contractions. In rare cases, contraction monitoring is performed internally. (If, perhaps, there's some difficulty obtaining an accurate reading from the external monitor.) As with internal fetal monitoring, your cervix must be dilated at least one centimeter and your membranes ruptured in order for the small, strawlike plastic monitoring device to be placed inside your uterus, between your uterine wall and the baby. This device not only monitors contractions very accurately, it provides a guide to the strength of contractions.

Just what is meconium anyway?

Meconium is the baby's first stool. It's a greenish substance from inside the baby's intestines, usually passed after the baby is born. Sometimes a baby passes meconium while he is still inside the uterus. This may be caused by stress, being overdue, or another medical problem. Meconium stains the amniotic fluid green. If meconium stained fluid is noted, your doctor may want to use internal fetal monitoring in order to monitor the baby more closely. Some doctors also dilute the amniotic fluid by flushing sterile saline solution into your uterus while you are laboring. During the delivery, the doctor will carefully suction the baby's nose and mouth to prevent the baby from breathing in the meconium.

More Hospital Worries

Going into the hospital is a strange experience, and many women fear the procedures, rules, and lack of control. Some moms-to-be, for example, want reassurance that they'll be allowed to eat during labor. The truth is, many women don't have much of an appetite because of the pain of contractions and nausea. If you are hungry, ask your doctor of midwife if you may eat a little something. Most healthcare providers will ask that you steer clear of solid foods and instead enjoy frozen juice bars, gelatin, and ice chips. That's because heavier foods might cause you to vomit during labor, and if you need an urgent C-section, it's safest to perform surgery on an empty stomach.

Will I need an enema?

Enemas are neither required nor routinely performed at the hospital. But did you know there's a very good chance you'll have a bowel movement during the pushing phase of labor? Doctors and nurses see it as a sign that you're pushing correctly. If the thought of having a bowel movement in front of others mortifies you, talk with your doctor about having an enema before delivery. Sometimes, healthcare providers suggest you perform it in the privacy of your home before your journey to hospital. Others will have a nurse assist you with an enema once you are there.

IVs and catheters

You might come across a couple of common medical devices in the hospital. The first is an intravenous (IV) line. A small needle is placed in a vein in your arm and a tiny catheter threaded through it. The needle is then removed. This line allows nurses to easily introduce fluids, pain medication, antibiotics, and other important substances into your system. Not every pregnant woman has an IV line, but most first-time moms generally end up with one. Ask your healthcare provider about her policy. You might also encounter a Foley catheter, a small tube placed in your urethra to keep your bladder drained. If you are able to get up during labor and use the bathroom, a Foley catheter may not be necessary. However, if you are having difficulty walking or cannot walk because of an epidural, a Foley catheter keeps your bladder empty. An empty bladder allows for better descent of the baby's head into the pelvis, so the nurse will probably want you to keep your bladder as empty as possible. Also, if you were to need a C-section, it's important that your bladder be empty because it could otherwise get in the way of the surgical field.

The big shave

Many women are curious about the shaving of pubic hair. In modern hospitals, women are no longer required to have their pubic hair shaved for a vaginal delivery. However, if you have a C-section, the top portion of pubic hair will be shaved to make room for the incision.

StAgEs Of LaBoR

First stage

The first stage of labor is known as the contraction phase. It begins when you start to experience painful, intense contractions that cause your cervix to dilate. It ends once your cervix is fully open to allow passage of the baby's head, when it is dilated 10 centimeters. This is the longest of all the stages of labor, typically lasting about 10 hours for a first-time mother and somewhat less for subsequent pregnancies. Sometimes, the first stage of labor is divided into subcategories—that is, early labor, when your cervix is dilated 1 to 3 centimeters; the active phase, when your cervix is 4 to 6 centimeters; and transition, from 7 to 9 centimeters.

Second stage

The second stage of labor is the pushing phase. It begins once your cervix is fully dilated 10 centimeters and ends with the delivery of the baby. Many women feel a great sense of relief when they are pushing. Perhaps after hours of contractions, it is a welcome relief to bear down and push the baby out. Plus, the pushing phase is great because you know you will soon be holding your baby in your arms. Most first-time mothers push for one to two hours. The time is considerably reduced with subsequent pregnancies. An epidural for pain relief may hamper the pushing phase because it sometimes blocks not only the pain-sensitive nerves, as it should, but also some of the muscles and nerves you need to push adequately. Usually this can be overcome with coaching from your partner and nurse. If not, the medication flowing through the epidural may be reduced so that you can push more effectively.

The cut that counts

An episiotomy is a small incision made by your doctor or midwife, usually during the pushing stage of labor. It starts in your vagina and extends downward toward your rectal area. The purpose is to extend and enlarge the perineal area for the passage of the baby's head. Lots of women are concerned about an episiotomy, but it's really no cause for alarm. Most healthcare providers don't cut anymore unless it seems absolutely necessary. Instead, the doctor or midwife uses various oils and lubricants to stretch and soften the perineum. The goal is to guide the baby's head through your perineum gently and without tears or cuts. Even if an episiotomy is necessary, your doctor or midwife may not make the decision until the baby's head is crowning (that is, bulging from the vagina). Only then can they adequately assess just how much the perineal tissue will stretch. For the episiotomy, the doctor or nurse numbs the area so there is no pain. After delivery, the doctor repairs the cut with absorbable sutures. An ice pack will be placed on your perineal area and pain medication provided. The discomfort is usually minimal. Ideally, it's best to have a vaginal delivery with no tears at all. But this may not always be possible, especially when delivering a first baby. If it appears that a large, jagged tear might occur, it may be preferable to have a straight, clean episiotomy cut because it is easier to repair and it heals best

Can self-massage help?

Some women practice stretching and lubricating their perineum during the last few weeks of pregnancy to extend and stretch the tissues and reduce the chance of tearing in the second stage (or the need for an episiotomy—see above). This practice doesn't work for everyone. Ask your doctor or midwife if preparation in advance would be beneficial for you.

Third stage

You may not even notice the third stage of labor because you'll be so preoccupied with your new baby. However, it's important because it delivers the placenta and membranes that supported the baby within your uterus. Once the baby has been delivered and the umbilical cord cut, the baby is handed to you and your partner. The nursery nurse hovers nearby, monitoring the baby. Meanwhile, your doctor or midwife deals with the remaining dangling umbilical cord and attached placenta and membranes. Typically within ten minutes or so, the placenta spontaneously detaches from your uterus and the attached umbilical cord remnant and membranes are delivered through your vagina. The placenta is about the size of an eight- or nine-inch pie or torte, but soft and malleable. You may not even notice its delivery, or you might experience a momentary, mild cramping or pressure sensation. Your healthcare provider then inspects your perineum and determines whether or not any repairs and sutures are needed. Then, you are cleansed and able to relax fully. Finally you can enjoy your new baby.

What happens to the placenta?

The placenta is the tissue that forms a nourishment link between mother and baby. It is attached to the inside of the uterus and is about the size of a single-layer, round cake. After the baby is born, the placenta spontaneously detaches from the uterus and is easily delivered through your vagina. Some cultures have some interesting uses for the placenta. In certain Native American traditions, the placenta is taken home and planted under a tree for good luck and prosperity. Some industrialized nations extract various nutrients from the placenta to be used in cosmetics and haircare products. It's not unknown for people to eat the placenta! It may be fried, roasted, or blended into a smoothie! Fortunately, you might think, most often in America the placenta is sent to the hospital incinerator and burned with the garbage.

PaIn MaNaGeMeNt

The pain of labor has been overly dramatized on television and in movies. The reality is that labor pain varies greatly from woman to woman and also from pregnancy to pregnancy. Some labors are quick and tolerable, and therefore pain relief may not be an important issue. Other labors seem to drag on for hour upon hour, and the pain and exhaustion demand that you take measures to make yourself more comfortable. It's a good idea to become familiar with pain-relief options before it gets to that point, and ideally before you even think about getting in the car to go to the hospital. That way, once labor has begun, you'll know what is offered and you'll be able to select the method that suits your situation best. Here is a brief synopsis of the options.

Natural/supportive methods

If you choose to have a completely natural delivery, more power to you. Most first-time mothers find this option isn't always feasible once the reality of painful contractions truly kick into high gear. Even so, it's certainly worth a try and you might find it very rewarding and successful. Having a baby in the natural way involves relying on measures other than medication for pain relief. They include breathing methods, relaxation techniques, focusing on objects, walking, showering, and taking a Jacuzzi—all can be helpful in dealing with the pain of labor contractions. It's best to have a supportive coach or partner assist you. The most successful natural births seem to have an active coach who gets right in the mother's face, breathing with her, and offering support and encouragement. The coach also provides massage and other ideas to get you through to the next contraction. This coach could be your partner, a friend, or a doula.

Pros and cons of natural techniques

✔ Avoid drugs and medication; thus, there are no risks to mother or baby.

✗ Do not always provide enough pain relief, particularly for first-time mothers, who may experience a longer labor than they had anticipated.

Local anesthesia

This method simply means an injection of numbing medication in your perineum as the baby comes through your vagina. As the baby's head descends through your vagina, the doctor or midwife injects numbing medication in your perineum. This numbs the vaginal area so that you don't feel discomfort as the baby passes through and is born.

Pros and cons of local anesthetic

✔ Almost no risks to you or the baby. The injected medication doesn't have time to affect the baby as she is being delivered, and it has little influence on your body because it is localized in your vaginal area. You are able to be completely alert and aware of your baby's delivery.

✗ You get pain throughout the great majority of your labor. This method provides relief only at the very end (when most women have stopped caring anyway).

real life pregnancy

"Give me drugs!"

"I wanted to experience a completely natural delivery and even hired a birthing hypnotist to help with pain management. I was doing well until I got to about 4 centimeters. At that point, the pain became so intense and relentless I screamed for real pain relief and fired the hypnotist on the spot. I needed an epidural right now. Within 20 minutes, the pain had gone. After my baby was born I felt a bit ashamed and disappointed, but both the doctor and nurse said I'd done a terrific job."

Carla, age 27

Narcotic medication

Many women find this method similar to the feeling of having a couple of cocktails. A narcotic medication such as Demerol is given through your IV line. This medication usually causes you to experience some sedation and sleepiness. You can still feel the contractions, but they may not seem quite so intense. You also don't seem to mind as much as you did before. Many women agree this technique takes the edge off the pain. It's often used when a woman feels she can almost make it, but just needs a little help to get through to the pushing stage.

Pros and cons of narcotics

✓ Provide moderate pain relief.

✗ You still experience some pain, and also feel somewhat sleepy and sedated.

✗ The medication crosses into the baby's circulation via the placenta. This is not typically a major problem because the baby is being monitored and your doctor can closely watch the baby's heartbeat.

✗ Your healthcare provider probably won't give you this type of medication within one hour of your estimated delivery (even if you scream for it). That's because the medication will still be in the baby's system when it is born and may cause the baby to be excessively drowsy.

Epidural

This regional "block" results in a temporary loss of feeling from the waist down—absolutely no pain during contractions or delivery. The epidural must be placed by a trained specialist, usually an anesthesiologist. A small area along your lower back is cleaned and numbed with an injection. Then a long, skinny needle is used to locate the space near your spinal cord. A tiny catheter tube is threaded into the space and the needle removed. Numbing medicine is injected through the catheter. Within a few minutes, you won't feel any pain from about the waist down. Medication is injected at regular intervals throughout your labor to keep you pain-free until you have delivered your baby. Sometimes, epidural medication is administered via an automatic pump, so you don't even have to ask for additional pain medication; it is automatically given to you.

Pros and cons of epidurals

✓ Outstanding pain relief. Epidurals are the best of all the pain-management options.

✓ Allows you to keep a clear head and enjoy the birth.

✗ Having the epidural catheter inserted is mildly uncomfortable.

✗ Because the procedure takes place in the sensitive area surrounding the spinal cord, there is a small chance of bleeding, infection, or leaking.

✗ There is a technical risk of paralysis. This is extremely rare, though. (I have delivered thousands of babies and have never seen this happen.)

✗ May make pushing difficult. If so, medication may be reduced during the pushing phase.

✗ Makes the use of forceps or vacuum more likely during the pushing phase because pushing may be too difficult with an epidural.

Entonox

In the United Kingdom, a gas (oxygen and nitrous oxide in equal measure) is inhaled by women in labor to help alleviate the pain of contractions. The baby suffers no ill effects, and Mom is in control of her pain relief.

Who chooses which pain management I'll use?

The choice of pain-relief medication is entirely up to you. Your doctor, midwife, and nurse will offer information and advice (and your partner, friends, and family may all have their say) but in the end, this is your birthing experience, your body, and your baby. Familiarize yourself with all the options, keep an open mind as labor progresses, and make your final decision once you know what the pain is like.

C-sEcTiOn

Just about everyone agrees that a vaginal delivery is the optimal choice for birthing a baby. But in some situations, it just may not be the safest or the best way to deliver your baby. In those circumstances, a Cesarean section (C-section) may offer you a safe alternative method of delivery. A C-section is a surgical method of delivering a baby through an incision made in the lower abdomen. In the United States, the C-section rate is about 25 percent. The rate is somewhat lower in most other countries. The most likely reason for the high C-section rate in the United States is the medical community's fear of a malpractice lawsuit. Unfortunately, the litigation threat is an enormous problem in the United States. If the doctor or nurse notes any questionable fetal monitor activity or any other uncertain problem, they will often cautiously opt for a C-section delivery.

The implications of C-sections

Like some women, you might know in advance that you will be delivering your baby by C-section. You or the baby might have a medical condition or other issue that dictates that a C-section is the safest method of delivery. This is great because you get time to get your head around the idea and plan for the practicalities. But more often than not, it seems, Cesarean sections are performed as an emergency procedure after some time of laboring. Here's what you need to know.

Pros and cons of C-sections

✓ You have a healthy baby, which may not be assured with a vaginal delivery.

✓ With a planned section you have time to plan child care and work commitments around the procedure.

✗ C-section is a major surgery and therefore has all the potential risks associated with surgery, such as infection and bleeding. Fortunately, this is a commonly performed surgery that is almost always accomplished without problems or complications.

✗ Longer recovery period for the mother than with a routine vaginal delivery.

✗ Some women feel disappointed that they didn't get to "give birth."

Pregnant thought

The method of your delivery is not as important as the well being of you and your baby. Whether you deliver vaginally or by C-section, the important goal is that you have the best birthing experience possible and that you and the baby are completely healthy and happy.

Planned C-sections

A Cesarean might be planned if you have one of the conditions detailed in the box. Your healthcare provider will advise on your own situation. Make sure you understand what's going on and ask all the questions you need to feel reassured that this is the right course for you. In special circumstances, your doctor may agree to try a vaginal delivery if you understand all the potential risks and benefits of each method of delivery. Typically, planned C-sections are scheduled about one week before your projected due date. This should be, we hope, before you go into labor spontaneously, and also when you are far enough along for your infant to be mature enough to be born. The nice feature about a planned C-section is that it is scheduled so well in advance that you and friends and family can plan around it. Work schedules and caring for other children can be prearranged. Friends and family can fly in to be with you and help out.

Reasons for a planned C-section

• The baby is in a breech position.

• The placenta is blocking the cervix, a condition known as placenta previa.

• You have maternal gestational diabetes (in some cases).

• You are expecting twins or more (in some cases).

• You have had a previous C-section, and declined an attempt at a vaginal birth.

• Herpes has broken out within 7 to 10 days of your projected due date.

Unplanned C-sections

It seems most C-sections are actually not planned. You probably experience some hours (days, even) of labor, then after a certain amount of time, it becomes evident that a vaginal delivery may not be the safest or most feasible way to deliver the baby.

Reasons for an unplanned C-section
- The baby seems distressed, or a non-reassuring fetal heartrate is displayed on the monitor.

- There is evidence on the fetal monitor that the umbilical cord is compressed (depleting the baby of oxygen).

- The baby is too large to fit through your pelvis.

- Labor contractions stop and your cervix fails to dilate any more.

What happens in surgery?

Your doctor and nurse fully explain the C-section procedure, outlining where the incision will be made (a low, horizontal cut just above your shaved pubic hair). Sometimes this incision is referred to as a "bikini-style" cut because it enables you to eventually wear your bikini and no one will ever notice your C-section scar. The surgery itself takes about one hour, and the expert medical team make sure you are comfortable and feel no pain during the procedure. Your doctor and an assistant perform the surgery. The assistant may be another physician, a trained midwife, or other trained surgical assistant. There will also be several nurses in the operating room to help out the medical team. And of course, the very important anesthesiologist physician will be near you to ensure you remain completely pain free.

Then what?

Most women stay in the hospital for several days after their C-section. For the first day or so you might feel quite uncomfortable, so pain medications are generously provided (if you want them). The baby stays in hospital with you during your entire stay. Once home, most women agree that they feel pretty much back to normal within a couple of weeks.

VbAc

VBAC stands for Vaginal Birth After C-section. A few short years ago, it seemed everyone was touting the praises of having a VBAC. Physicians frequently counseled patients that a repeat C-section was not required just because they delivered their first babies by C-section. In fact, physicians often encouraged patients to try for a vaginal delivery for their second birthing experience. The old-fashioned adage, "Once a C-section, always a C-section" was thrown out. Yet now, just a couple of years later, things seemed to have changed somewhat and the old pendulum is swinging back to repeat C-sections once again. VBACs may still be an option, but they are no longer looked upon as risk-free or widely encouraged by all physicians. Some women like having a VBAC because they want to experience a vaginal delivery. Others prefer a repeat C-section because it can be scheduled ahead of time and it takes the worry out of going through labor. It's a complex issue with no rights and wrongs. If you have had a previous C-section, be sure to talk with your doctor, and work together to determine which delivery method is best for you and your baby.

Why the turnaround?

The recent lack of popularity of VBAC comes because some recent medical research studies show that a woman with a previous C-section scar on her uterus is at a higher risk of uterine rupture (scar separation) than once thought. Although uterine rupture is still fairly unlikely, it gives us pause to consider the advantages and disadvantages of VBAC versus having a repeat C-section.

Pros and cons of VBAC

✓ You avoid major surgery and all the associated risks.

✓ Recovery from a vaginal delivery is considerably easier and a lot shorter.

✓ Family and friends can be more involved and participate in a vaginal delivery.

✗ There is a remote risk of a previous C-section scar separating and the uterus rupturing.

✗ You may attempt a vaginal delivery and not be successful, ending up with a repeat C-section after all.

What you need to know

Any conversation between you and your healthcare provider discussing the merits and disadvantages of VBAC versus repeat C-section should always include a look at why you had your initial C-section in the first place. For example, if it was because your eight-pound baby couldn't fit through your pelvis, and you're pregnant again with another estimated eight-pound baby, it may be best to schedule the repeat C-section. However, if your initial C-section occurred because your first baby was in a breech position, and your second baby is not, you might want to explore your VBAC options. Similarly if your first C-section was ordered because of fetal distress, herpes outbreak, twins, or an abnormal placenta, these situations are not as likely to recur with the second pregnancy, making you a better bet for a VBAC.

It's also important to consider the type of incision made on your uterus during your first C-section. It doesn't necessarily match your skin incision. If your doctor didn't specifically tell you which type of uterine incision you received, your current doctor may need to request a copy of your previous C-section operative report. If a vertical incision was made on your uterus, you will almost assuredly be required to have a repeat C-section. That's because the risk of scar separation and uterine rupture is more than ten times that of a horizontal incision. If you find your uterine incision was made horizontally, you may be a candidate for a VBAC. There is a still a slight chance of scar separation and uterine rupture, but the chances are significantly more remote.

Mother of the future?

Another important consideration when discussing a VBAC is your future childbearing plans. If you desire many more children, a VBAC may be more attractive. That might lead to more vaginal deliveries and avoid multiple repeat C-sections. On the other hand, if your childbearing days are over, you might want to opt for the repeat C-section. You might even want to have your tubes tied during the operation! A tubal ligation cuts and ties your Fallopian tubes and provides permanent sterilization. That should never be performed unless you are completely sure that you do not want to bear more children. If you elect to have a tubal ligation with your repeat C-section, talk with your doctor—and your partner, of course. Various consents need to be signed ahead of time. The tubal ligation procedure is quite simple when performed in tandem with a C-section (an additional five minutes), with relatively no additional risk or complications.

Third Trimester Letter

To Mommy from Baby

Dear Mommy,

Hello again, Mommy. This will be my last letter before I get to meet you in person. When I think about being held closely in your arms, I can hardly wait to be born.

Fortunately, we don't have to wait much longer. As of today, I'm 35 weeks old and weigh about five and a half pounds. Even if I was born today, I'd probably do well. But I suppose it's best for me to wait a little while longer.

In case you didn't know yet, my head is already down and in position for my big delivery journey. Sorry if it's causing some added pressure on your bladder. But being in position is a good thing: It means my birthday is quickly approaching. Hooray!

I've been meaning to tell you that it's terrific how you've been exercising a couple of times each week. I especially enjoy our yoga class. It really helps me with my stretching and positioning. It also provides soothing comfort. Don't you agree, Mommy? I hope we can continue to do fun activities like yoga together after I'm born, too.

Oh, I have one more important question to ask you. Do we have a doggie? I thought I heard barking the other night. Is that our dog or just the neighbors? I'm hoping that it's ours because I think it would be great to have a doggie. I know you'll make sure that the dog and I are properly introduced and become fast friends.

That's really all for now. You'll be holding and cuddling me soon. Yippee!

Always lots of hugs and kisses for you,

Your Little Love

CHAPTER 9

So What Now?

Junior's First Test

Within minutes of your baby being born, you'll hear the doctors and nurses calling out numbers. Many women mistakenly think these figures indicate the weight of the baby. More often than not, the numbers being discussed are your newborn baby's Apgar scores. The Apgar system is a method of evaluating the overall health status of your newborn baby. If you become a little more familiar with the scoring system, you might even be able to decipher what they're talking about. Babies typically receive two sets of scores. One set of scores is given at one minute of life; the next at five minutes of life. Occasionally, a third set will be given at the ten-minute milestone; however, that's usually reserved for premature or high-risk infants. In general, the higher the score, the better the newborn baby's condition. The baby is judged and scored in five areas.

What babies are scored on

Heart rate

- Above 100 beats per minute—score 2 points.
- Heart rate is less than 100 beats per minute—score 1 point.
- Heart rate is absent —score 0 points.

Muscle tone

- Active and moving—score 2 points.
- Some movement observed—score 1 point.
- Not moving, limp—score 0 points.

Respiratory effort

- Crying and breathing well—score 2 points.
- Breathing somewhat irregular or slow—score 1 point.
- Not breathing—score 0 points.

Reflexes

- Vigorous reflexes and response to stimulus—score 2 points.
- Some reaction to stimulation —score 1 point.
- Does not respond to stimulus—score 0 points.

Color

- Coloring is entirely pink— score 2 points.
- Body is pink, but hands and feet are blue—score 1 point.
- Coloring is pale or blue—score 0 points.

Assessing baby's score

Each category in the Apgar test scores 0, 1, or 2 points. The highest score available is 2 points making a total perfect score of 10. The score assigned is a reflection of how well the baby is doing. For example, if the baby did perfectly in a category, a score of 2 would be assigned. A 1 assigned in a category shows that the baby is doing fairly well, and a 0 indicates that a baby is doing poorly. If the baby scores perfectly in all five categories, she receives a round 10—pretty rare for a newborn. (In fact, there is an old joke that only doctors' and nurses' babies are allowed to receive a perfect 10.) Most babies receive Apgar scores in the range of 7 to 9, which reflects how they are adapting to the new conditions outside the womb.

The second set of scores at five minutes may be somewhat higher, showing that the baby is quickly adapting to life in her new environment. For example, a baby who scored seven and then nine might have been quiet and suppressed initially in her breathing (score 0) but by five minutes crying and yelling in a healthy, robust manner (score 2). You'll hear the nurse shout, "This baby is a 7/9" to let the medical team know how well the baby is doing. The figures will be written into the baby's medical record.

Fascinating fact

Since you now understand Apgar scores, also know this: The baby is weighed within the first half hour of life. The nurse usually lets you know that it's about to happen so your partner can take a photo of junior's first big weigh-in.

Fascinating fact

Most newborn babies miss receiving that perfect Apgar score of ten because of the color category. It seems most newborns have fully pink bodies but still have tinges of blue in their hands and feet. That's because in the first few minutes outside the womb, the baby is hard at work pumping blood to all areas of the body. Miraculously, the baby is already smart enough to circulate blood to important organs such as the heart and the brain, leaving the fingers and toes last to receive the lifegiving liquid. Within a day or so, the baby will be completely pink.

real life pregnancy

"We know his lucky number."

"My baby boy just shot out; the birth was incredibly easy. Then I heard the nurses yelling out, "This baby is a 9/9." I just assumed that 9/9 was his weight. The doctor shook his head and explained in a kind of patronizing way that 9/9 was his Apgar scores. About an hour later, the nurse took the time to weigh the little guy. Guess what he weighed? 9 pounds and 9 ounces. He truly was 9/9 and 9/9."

Vicky, age 18

Bank That Blood

The blood remaining in your baby's umbilical cord after delivery is rich in a special type of cell called stem cells. Stem cells are "master cells" that are able to produce other cells found in the blood and immune systems. These cells can be collected easily at the time of delivery and cryo-preserved (a freezing technique) in case they are needed later in life. Stem cells are currently being used to treat almost 100 different life-threatening illnesses, especially cancers, leukemia, and multiple types of blood disorders. And they may prove useful in the treatment of other diseases as medical research develops. Naturally, the blood is a guaranteed match for your baby. It also has about a one-in-four chance of being a match for a sibling. Other family members are at somewhat lower odds, but research studies show that using cord blood from a relative in a medical procedure doubles the survival rate compared to treatment from an unrelated donor. Some parents choose to collect and store their baby's cord blood so those stem cells could be used by the baby or another family member in case of future serious illness. Other parents believe the chance of ever needing a baby's cord blood is remote and not worth the hassle or expense.

Whose call is it?

The decision to bank your baby's umbilical cord blood is entirely yours. Although it's always wise to hear what your doctor, family, and close friends have to say on the matter, ultimately, this is a personal decision based on your beliefs, financial situation, and family medical history. You have to make the decision before your baby is born.

Pros and cons of umbilical cord banking

✓ Guaranteed match for the baby.

✓ One-in-four chance of a match for a sibling.

✓ Many studies show how successful medical treatment using these cells can be.

✓ Collecting cord blood is easy, without pain or complications to mother or baby.

✓ Can be stored for decades.

✗ Rather costly—the initial set-up fee is about $1,500, with an annual storage fee of about $100.

✗ Must be arranged well in advance and the blood-collection kit brought to the delivery and mailed the next day.

✗ Blood might be collected and stored but never used.

✗ The blood may not be a match for a family member in need.

How do we go about it?

The process is quite simple. You make the arrangements ahead of time with the cord-banking company of your choice. The company sends a collection kit for you to take to the delivery room, plus a set of detailed instructions. Just let your delivery nurse and doctor know and they will do the rest. The cord blood is easily collected by your doctor shortly after the baby has been born. The nurse securely packs the blood into the kit, a few papers are signed, and you mail the completed package according to the instructions. The company files the blood in its cryogenic (freezing) storage facilities. It's not known exactly how long blood can be frozen and stored, but studies have shown that stem cells are viable for more than 15 years.

BrEaSt Or BoTtLe?

Nature's perfect food, breast milk, contains the best nutrients for your baby and is the standard that formula milks are judged against. However, many outstanding infant formulas are available that do an excellent job of providing your baby with nutrients, vitamins, and minerals. Most women choose to breast-feed, if only for a short period of time. However, some women do not wish to nurse for personal reasons and might feel hassled by nurses and other members of the healthcare team. There is no right or wrong way to feed your baby; you decide what works best for your circumstances. Talk with your doctor, the baby's doctor, your close friends and family, a lactation expert, and other new mothers to help you decide which choice is best for you and your baby.

Pros and cons of breast-feeding

✓ The best nutrition available for babies.

✓ Protects babies from infections.

✓ Costs little or nothing.

✓ Very easy and convenient after the first stressful weeks.

✓ You get your figure back quicker.

✓ May reduce your risk of getting cancer.

✓ Promotes bonding and intimacy with baby.

✗ You might have to avoid certain foods, drinks, and medications.

✗ You might feel cramping and pain in the uterus for the first few days.

✗ Breasts can become engorged, painful, or infected.

✗ Can be difficult to establish without expert help (e.g., some mothers fear they don't have sufficient milk).

✗ You often leak milk, even on hearing or seeing a baby.

Pros and cons of bottle-feeding

✓ Excellent nutritional formulas are available, and you can choose from cow or soy, ready-made or powder.

✓ No pain or physical discomfort (other than having to make up bottles at night).

✓ Others can help out with baby's feedings, giving you much-needed rest.

✓ Easy to carry out in most public places.

✓ You can eat, drink, and take whatever meds you want.

✗ No protection against infection for baby.

✗ Equipment must be sterilized and bottles prepared, mixed, and warmed.

✗ Costly—from $1,500 to $4,000 annually.

✗ You lose pregnancy weight more slowly.

✗ Others may criticize you.

✗ You may need to switch formulas until you find a brand that suits your baby.

Choosing To Breast-feed

It's easiest to learn how to breast-feed while still in the hospital, where nurses and lactation consultants are available to help get you started. They have numerous tricks up their sleeve to assist you in your endeavor (and sometimes you need to be persistent in trying them out over and again until you and baby get it right). You might be able to set up an appointment with experts outside the hospital, but this will be at your own expense. Some moms decide to try breast-feeding and, if it doesn't work out, switch to formula. Others swear that all that fussing with sterilizers and lost pacifiers is far more wearisome than getting over the initial pain and wakeful nights nursing inevitably brings. The most important thing is that you are comfortable with your decision and that you and your baby remain healthy.

When do I start feeding the baby?

Assuming the baby is doing well, is alert and ready to suck, most babies are crying for a first feed within a few hours of delivery. Babies who are particularly small or large may need to be fed within the first one or two hours, so it's best to have made a decision about feeding methods before arriving at the hospital for the delivery.

Breast-feeding in public?

From time to time, this makes the news and causes a bit of a stir. Some argue that breast-feeding is a natural event and that a baby must be fed when hungry. Others say that it's distasteful to show your breasts in public. Go ahead and feed your baby as you see fit. It may be "politically correct" to tastefully drape a cloth or shawl over your shoulder and breast during the feeding. That way, your baby is properly fed and you limit the gawkers and unwanted stares.

Are there special things I need to do?

The best news? When breast-feeding, you need to consume an additional 300 to 500 calories above your normal nonpregnant diet. The not-so-good news? You can't make them up entirely of chocolate and savory snacks, much as you might crave them while nursing. It's vitally important at this time for you (and your baby) to eat a well-balanced diet. You also need to drink plenty of fluids and continue taking your prenatal vitamins. You might find that certain foods and drinks disagree with your infant: Spicy foods or certain vegetables, such as cabbage, can sometimes cause the baby to be extra gassy or have stomach upset. After a short time, you'll figure out which foods the baby can tolerate. Of course, alcohol is off limits, too, because it can pass through to the baby.

Ouch!

You may notice that your nipples are quite sore and tender when you first begin breast-feeding. This usually goes away within a couple of weeks. You could try applying a little olive oil or calendula cream on your nipples after each feeding session to help alleviate the soreness. Other moms swear by savoy cabbage leaves (place them inside your bra). In a few weeks, your breasts will become accustomed to nursing and the soreness will go away.

Pump that milk

Some working mothers face an added challenge. How do you continue breast-feeding while away from baby? Many women purchase breast pumps or rent them from the hospital or a medical supply company, and spend lunch hours sitting in the bathroom trying to collect milk to store (in the work fridge or freezer) to take home for baby's feedings the next day. It can be tedious (but sometimes better than leaking tell-tale circles on your sweater during important meetings). Other mothers find they can breast-feed at home and have the caregiver feed the baby formula while they are at work.

Mythbusting

The myth: If you don't breast-feed your baby, you're not a good mom.

The truth: Feeding your baby is just a small part of motherhood. If you choose to bottle-feed your baby for personal or career reasons, it is absolutely *not* a reflection on your mothering abilities. You can be a wonderful, loving, and caring mother no matter how you choose to feed your baby.

Circumcision Decision

If you delivered a boy baby, you will be asked whether or not you'd like to have your new son circumcised. A circumcision is the removal of the foreskin that shields the head of the penis. The decision is totally up to you and your partner. When making your decision, you'll want to consider your cultural, religious, and ethnic traditions. You should also consider whether the baby's dad or siblings are circumcised, because most families like to have a matching set.

Pros and cons of circumcision

✔ Easier to clean, improved hygiene.

✔ May match dad and brothers.

✔ Reduced risk of infection.

✔ Ancient cultural and religious ritual.

✘ Not medically necessary.

✘ Painful procedure for the baby.

✘ Risk to baby during surgery.

✘ Costly, and may not be covered by insurance.

Expert opinion

The American Academy of Pediatrics came out with an opinion on circumcision in 1999. They stated that the benefits are not significant enough to recommend circumcision as a routine procedure. That's why insurance companies are choosing no longer to cover the procedure as medically necessary surgery.

What happens?

If you decide to have your baby circumcised, the procedure is generally done the day after birth while you are still in the hospital. It is usually performed by your baby's doctor. In Jewish tradition, circumcision is performed one week after the birth by a specially trained religious person called a *mohel*. The procedure itself only takes a few minutes. Before the procedure, be sure to ask the doctor or mohel about your baby's pain management. Some doctors use no pain medication whatsoever. Others apply either a topical numbing medication to the penis or inject a numbing nerve block to the baby's pubic region.

After the circumcision, you'll be given instructions on how to care for the circumcised penis at home. Typically, parents keep the area clean with a gentle soap and water. Petroleum jelly is often recommended to prevent the skin from sticking to the baby's diaper. The circumcision usually heals within a week or two. Your baby's doctor will be sure to examine the area at baby's first doctor visit.

real life pregnancy

"My poor baby boy."

"I knew I was having a baby boy, but was really undecided about circumcision. Of course, my husband wanted to have the procedure performed because he'd been circumcised himself. He thought it looked better and was better from a hygiene standpoint. I knew where he was coming from, but worried about hurting my tiny newborn when it wasn't absolutely necessary. I went on my own to speak with the baby's pediatrician, who said the procedure was safe and promised to use adequate pain relief. I agreed to have him circumcised, and boy was daddy happy!"

Janet, age 34

Postpartum Primer

Once you've delivered your baby, you may look forward to the return of your old self. But after undergoing so many changes during the past 40 weeks or so, your body and mind might have other ideas. Your belly won't magically spring back into shape after the third stage of labor; nor will your memory, levels of energy, and emotions be where they were the night you conceived. But with lots of care and time, you will be looking and feeling more like your old self.

But I'm still overweight!

Your body went through extreme physical changes during pregnancy. Little by little, it will begin the move back to its pre-pregnancy state. Your abdominal muscles, for instance, will firm up over time, especially if you help things along with moderate exercise after you've had your six-week check.

Period pains?

Your uterus was larger than a basketball at the time of delivery. It's amazing to realize that within six weeks of delivery it's returned to the size of a pear. This usually doesn't come without a little pain. As your uterus shrinks back into place, you'll probably experience some cramping and bleeding. The cramping lasts only a few days and can be controlled with mild pain medication (though it worsens with each birth and with breast-feeding). The bleeding is typically heavy for a few days and eventually slows to a light period. Your doctor or midwife will probably suggest you wear sanitary pads instead of tampons because of the risk of infection. After a few weeks (six weeks isn't unusual), all vaginal bleeding and discharge will stop.

Pain in the butt

Your perineum (the area between your vagina and rectum) may be somewhat swollen or bruised right after delivery. It may be especially tender if you experienced a tear or episiotomy. If you're finding it uncomfortable to urinate, try sitting in a basin of warm water. The perineal area reacts much like the tissue inside your mouth. For example, if you accidentally bite the inside of your mouth, it's sore for a day or two, but then it quickly heals without a trace of a lesion or tear. Your perineum heals in much the same way. Your doctor or midwife may also order soothing foam or spray for your aching bottom. These products typically contain a mild numbing medication that can provide relief to a bruised, torn perineum. Ask your doctor if this is an option for you.

Swollen breasts

You know how your breasts become tender and enlarged during pregnancy? Within a day or two of delivery, they engorge even more as your breast milk comes in. They may temporarily feel uncomfortably full, firm, and tender. If you are breast-feeding, the act of nursing your baby releases the milk and relieves the symptoms. (You'll be on the verge of waking the baby for feeding.) If you decide not to breast-feed, you may be uncomfortable for a day or so until the milk dissipates. Be sure to wear a tight bra, apply ice packs to your breasts, and take an over-the-counter pain medication. Within a couple of days, your breast milk will be gone and you'll be feeling just fine.

JuST LeT mE sLeEp!

It's completely normal to feel the most tired you've ever felt in the first few days after birth. After all, you've just completed a pregnancy and delivered a baby, a monumental mental and physical accomplishment (don't forget to keep reminding your man). Add to the mix physical factors such as changing hormones and, of course, your new baby waking you at various times throughout the night for feeding, and it's no surprise you're at your wit's end. Newborns don't sleep for long intervals; they usually wake every few hours to eat. Do know that this eventually gets much better. In the meantime, use the suggestions here to help you through.

How to feel better

- Sleep, or at least try to rest, whenever the baby does.
- Eat a well-balanced diet.
- Continue your prenatal vitamins.
- Forget perfection; do only what is absolutely necessary around the house.
- Share your thoughts with other mothers in the same situation.
- Ask for help from friends and family.
- Try to get some moderate exercise each week.
- Get outside at least once a day for some fresh air.
- Pamper yourself: Take a bubble bath, get a manicure, buy something frivolous.

The moody blues

Many women find they experience emotional changes after delivery. In fact, seven out of ten mothers experience some degree of postpartum blues or anxiety. These feelings typically occur about a week of so after delivery, and are brought on by the drastic drop in hormones, your lack of sleep, and overall life changes. Some women feel sad, crying for no apparent reason, or feel restless, irritable, or anxious. Many women even report wondering if having a baby was such a good idea. Reassure yourself that such thoughts are completely normal and many women have them. It is absolutely no reflection on the type of mother you are. Fortunately, these feelings and thoughts almost always go away as quickly as they came. Occasionally, a more serious form of emotions occurs, called postpartum depression. It's similar to the blues and anxiety, but it is more intense and lasts considerably longer.

The blues aren't lifting

About 10 percent of women experience postpartum depression. This is a condition that lasts longer and has more serious symptoms than "the blues." You may be more prone to postpartum depression if you have experienced depression in the past or it runs in your family. Women who had a difficult time conceiving or experienced a particularly stressful, difficult pregnancy may also be more likely to experience postpartum depression. If you think that might be happening to you, please talk with your doctor right away. There are anti-depressant medications and counseling groups that can be used temporarily to help you feel more like your old self again.

Your Six-week Check

If you've had a C-section delivery, you'll have an appointment with your healthcare provider two weeks after delivery and again in another four weeks. If you've had an uncomplicated vaginal delivery, you will have an appointment with your doctor or midwife approximately six weeks after delivering your baby. It's an important visit and a great opportunity to share your thoughts and concerns about everything you've been through, good and bad. Your healthcare provider will perform a thorough physical examination to ensure that all of you is healing and getting back to normal. The doctor or midwife will also ask how you are feeling and how you are handling the new responsibilities of motherhood. This is an excellent time to voice any worries. Be sure to speak up if something is on your mind (your doctor will have heard it all before).

Back to birth control!

It's at this appointment that your doctor brings up the topic of birth control. (Yes, women have been known to have sex again after birth; some have even found out they are pregnant again at their six-week check.) Even if you are breast-feeding solely, you can get pregnant. After examining your vagina to check that you've healed, your doctor will give the go ahead to return to normal physical activities. You won't need to schedule another office visit until you are due for your next pelvic examination, usually either in six months or a year, depending on your doctor. That is, of course, unless you become pregnant again and get to do it all over again.

CHAPTER 10
DaDdY
BoOt CaMp

Your Changing Body

You heard that right. Every dad-to-be goes through some pretty odd changes, too. Some men truly do experience food cravings, appetite changes, nausea, and other physical symptoms. Men's response to pregnancy can be just as varied and strange as women's. It's most often an emotional change, but we've all heard tales of men whose waistbands expand alongside their pregnant wives'. It's like sympathy weight gain—and don't think women don't relish it. What a bonding experience for both of you to go from regular size clothing to XXL comfy pants.

Second that emotion

When you first heard the news about the pregnancy, what did you think? You wouldn't be a real man if your happiness wasn't laced with doubt. It's perfectly normal for excitement and hope to bring on confusion and fear. You may need to take some time out to reflect on your many conflicting emotions.

The good ...

When you hear the baby's heartbeat for the first time, you will most likely be amazed and overjoyed. What pride to hear your son's or daughter's heart beating inside the womb. And seeing your baby on ultrasound is nothing short of a miracle. Try to go along to appointments with your partner. These experiences really heighten your sense of reality and reinforce that the baby is truly on the way, especially when you have concerns about your new role. Attending childbirth classes is also vitally important in building your role as a father and supportive coach.

. . . the bad

Admit it. Sometimes you just feel overwhelmed with all the changes, and nervous about your added responsibilities. Be sure to share these concerns with other fathers-to-be you meet at class. Talk also to dads who have gone through the birth process and survived the early weeks and months. Chances are, they all feel or felt many of the same emotions as you.

. . . and the not so ugly

Just as you become accustomed to the pregnancy, it's time to welcome the baby into your world. That gives rise to a whole new flood of perhaps unwelcome feelings. Not to worry. You know you're going to be a terrific dad: You wouldn't be reading this right now if you weren't such a concerned and caring person. How lucky for your wife and new baby that you play such an important part in their lives. This is all going to work out great!

Man trouble

Of course every guy is individual, but you'd be amazed at how commonly the same issues come up as a source of conflict for men contemplating becoming dads. Here are some of the most common anxieties.

My partner's becoming someone else

One of the chief concerns many dads-to-be have is watching a partner adjust to the changes of pregnancy. Even though women have been going through these changes for millennia (or you wouldn't be here), it can be unnerving to find your wife so uncomfortable, fatigued, or ill-tempered. Do you wonder how to help? The most important thing you can do is be supportive and encouraging. Her body and emotions are doing weird things, and even if you don't completely understand what she's going through, do your absolute best to be kind, sweet, and understanding. There may be times when her actions make no sense whatsoever to you. That's to be expected. Just do your best to hang in there and try to be as encouraging and empathetic as you can.

Should I be doing something?

When it comes to decision-making and planning for the pregnancy and childbirth, make sure your wife gets 51 percent of the vote. Of course, your input is important, but in most cases, these decisions really affect her more than you. But do stay involved in all the plans and preparations for your new arrival. It's a good way for you to get to understand more about what your wife and the baby are going through. It may also help you to understand what is going on inside your own head.

Money mAtTeRs

It's absolutely normal to have financial concerns in the run-up
to the birth of a baby. Traditionally, it has been the man in the
relationship who feels a strong sense of financial responsibility.
That may or may not be the case in your family. But at any rate,
pregnancy can bring up important questions about money and
financial planning. Let the questions in the box prompt you to
start thinking about the issues. Of course it's important to have
a good handle on your new financial situation. But try to keep
it in perspective and don't become preoccupied with financial
worries. Talk openly with your wife about money matters.
Together you can come up with a financial plan that works best
for your situation.

Questions to ask

- Will you both continue to work?
- If one of you stays home, how will that affect the household budget?
- Will you need to hire a nanny or caregiver?
- Will you need to move to a larger home?
- Is your car big enough and safe enough for a baby?

real life pregnancy

"Not now, please."

"I was stunned when my wife announced she was pregnant. Although we'd been married two years, we planned to wait for kids until we both finished law school. Instead, this unplanned pregnancy was happening right in the middle of our professional education. We had heated discussions about how a baby would affect school, jobs, and our finances before devising a plan to share the responsibilities and set aside some money for child care and a part-time nanny. Once that got sorted, I relaxed a bit and even started looking forward to becoming a dad."

Ryan, age 32

ThE sEx ThInG

Granted, this is a tough topic. After all, sex is what got you pregnant in the first place. It's not unusual for women to change how they feel about sex (from hour to hour, even) when they get pregnant. Some women get extra sexy during pregnancy, perhaps as a result of changing hormones. If this is your wife, go with it and give thanks. However, most women experience a decrease in sexual appetite, especially in the first few weeks after finding out about the pregnancy, and certainly after giving birth, and while having to cope with an infant who wakes frequently at night (if someone demanded you get out of bed every couple hours for 18 months, your libido would plummet, too). Accept that she just may just not be in the mood for romance for a while. Even if she is emotionally ready, the physical demands of pregnancy might get in the way. Her breasts might be incredibly tender and sensitive, or she may feel self-conscious about her expanding body. The best thing you can do is to be as patient and understanding as you can.

What if I don't feel like it?

Sometimes it's the man who finds his expectations and attitudes about sex shift during pregnancy. You might feel anxious about having sex because you're concerned about hurting the baby, or worry that the baby is spying on you. If the pregnancy is a normal, low risk pregnancy, there's no reason to abstain from sex. The baby is well protected within the womb and won't be hurt. She also has no idea of what you're up to!

Oedipus and all that

Some men feel odd having sex with someone who's going to be a mother. They've always associated the act with young, sexy women, not someone they can connect with their own mother. Although that's perfectly understandable, you might think about the ways in which pregnancy actually enhances your relationship. Perhaps it adds another layer of depth and maturity, for instance. Your partner will be a mother and you'll be a father. Together you have created this wonderful, precious new baby. That's pretty sexy in its own right, don't you think?

WhAt kiNd of DaD wiLl i bE?

Will becoming a dad change the man you are now? How will
others view you? How might it change your relationship with
your wife or your own parents? Making the transition from man
to father is a step into the unknown. These thoughts may help.

Man to man

Some men express concerns that they don't want to be like their own
fathers. Your own father may or may not serve as a good role model
for the type of dad you'd like to be. Keep in mind that the role of
fatherhood changes from generation to generation. Today's father is
quite different from the dad of twenty or thirty years ago. Your role
as dad is influenced by society and the times, and also by the needs
of your own family. If possible, chat with your father about his way of
parenting. What did he enjoy most? What would he do differently if he
had the opportunity again? Such a discussion could provide insight and
thoughtful ideas as you imagine yourself as a father.

Togetherness

Of course, you'll want to discuss your concerns about your impending
new role with your partner. After all, you'll need her mothering
philosophy and your fathering skills to work together as a team.
Child-rearing works best when you share similar styles. After the baby
arrives, you can work together to adjust to your new circumstances.
Once done, try to relax and enjoy this new part of your life, day to day.

Mythbusting

The myth: The men in your family aren't actively involved or openly emotional with their children, so you won't be either.

The truth: Times have changed. Most women today are attracted to a man who displays open emotions and expresses his love for his children. Plus, in our modern world of two-income marriages, more and more dads are taking an active role in their children's daily activities. Take a stab at it. You'll be rewarded with the tremendous joy and happiness that comes with being a terrific father to your children.

Pregnant thought

One hundred years from now, it won't matter what your bank account was, the type of house you lived in, or the kind of car you drove ... but the world may be better because you were important in the life of a child.

PlAn Of AcTiOn

If you're like many men, you'll want to have a concrete, practical plan of action to follow through the pregnancy and upcoming delivery. So here it is, as plain and simple as can be. Follow these guidelines and the pregnancy and delivery should be smooth sailing, and you and your partner will discover incredible joy and satisfaction in sharing the parenting of your precious baby.

During pregnancy

- Become involved with the pregnancy; know what is going on with your partner and the baby.
- If possible, go with your partner to her doctor visits—you'll learn a lot and have some fun, too.
- Understand that your partner needs some extra tender loving care.
- Your partner is growing and needs more than half of the bed, so move over, man.
- Spend time alone as a couple just talking and expressing your hopes and fears.
- Give your woman as much support, encouragement, and love as you can.
- Surprising her with a special little gift now and then will have amazing results.
- Plan a special date night at least once a week—and keep this up even after the baby arrives.
- Keep reassuring your partner about what a wonderful mother she is going to be.
- Take some time alone to reflect on your feelings about becoming a new father.

- Talk with other fathers-to-be or new fathers and get as many tips as you can.
- Go to the bookstore and buy a book on parenting that suits your particular interests.
- Play an active role in childbirth classes and learn as much as possible.
- Take a tour of where the baby will be born.
- Work with your partner to get things ready for the baby, such as furniture and stocking the nursery.

During delivery

- When it comes to the delivery, be actively present and share the joy of birthing together.
- During the birth, tell you partner what a terrific job she is doing and how much you love her.

Once the baby arrives

- See if you can take a little time off from work.
- After the baby is born, understand that your position as center of your partner's universe has been severely dislocated, but please don't take it personally.
- Understand that you cannot compete for attention with the baby.
- Try to share baby care responsibilities and help out with your baby whenever possible.

How do you feel?

Use the following pages to chart your feelings, the changes in your body, and your hopes and anxieties in the weeks of your pregnancy.

Week 1

Week 2

Week 3

Week 4

Week 5

Week 6

Week 7

Week 8

Week 9

Week 10

Week 11

Week 12

Week 13

_____

_____

_____

_____

_____

Week 14

_____

_____

_____

_____

_____

Week 15

_____

_____

_____

_____

_____

_____

Week 16

Week 17

Week 18

Week 19
_____

Week 20
_____

Week 21
_____

Week 22

Week 23

Week 24

Week 25

Week 26

Week 27

Week 28

Week 29

Week 30

Week 31
_____

Week 32
_____

Week 33
_____

Week 34

Week 35

Week 36

Week 37

Week 38

Week 39

Week 40

ReSoUrCeS

Web sites

Sidelines National Support Network
Information and support for high-risk or complicated pregnancies
http://www.sidelines.org/

Just for Mom
Information, inspiration, and encouragement for moms
http://www.justformom.com/

Single Mothers
Support for single mothers
http://www.singlemothers.org/

Share: Pregnancy & Infant Loss Support
Provides pregnancy and infant loss support
http://www.nationalshareoffice.com/

Miscarriage Support
Helps women and their families cope with miscarriage
http://www.miscarriagesupport.org/

My Local Pregnancy
Resource guide for pregnant women in local areas across the United States
http://www.mylocalpregnancy.com/

U.S. Consumer Product Safety Commission
Health and safety for consumer products, including baby products
http://www.cpsc.gov/

Pregnancy and Baby
Information and resources for preconception, pregnancy, birth, and baby
http://www.pregnancyandbaby.com/

Healthy Pregnancy
Information from The National Women's Health Information Center
http://www.4woman.gov/pregnancy

BabyCenter
New and expectant parent resource guide and newsletter
http://www.babycenter.com/

iVillage
Forum for women's health issues including pregnancy and parenting
http://www.ivillage.com/

Amazing Pregnancy
Pregnancy information, week by week guide, picture gallery
http://www.amazingpregnancy.com/

The American College of
Obstetricians and Gynecologists
http://www.acog.org/

American College of Nurse-
Midwives
http://www.midwife.org/

Doulas of North America
http://www.dona.org/

American Academy of Pediatrics
http://www.aap.org/

La Leche League
Breast-feeding and nutritional
information
http://www.lalecheleague.org/

Books

*Countdown to Baby: Answers to the
100 Most Asked Questions about
Pregnancy and Childbirth*, Susan
Warhus, M.D., Addicus Books, 2003

The Womanly Art of Breastfeeding,
La Leche League International,
Plume, 2004

*Down Came the Rain: My Journey
through Postpartum Depression*,
Brooke Shields, Hyperion, 2005

*After the Baby's Birth . . . A Women's
Way to Wellness: A Complete Guide
for Postpartum Women*, Robin Lim,
Celestial Arts, 1991

*The Baby Book: Everything You Need
to Know About Your Baby from Birth
to Age Two*, William Sears and
Martha Sears, Little, Brown, 2003

*The Diaper Diaries: The Real Poop
on a New Mom's First Year*, Cynthia
L. Copeland, Workman Publishing
Company, 2003

*Ready or Not . . . Here We Come!
The Real Experts' Cannot-Live-
Without Guide to the First Year with
Twins*, Elizabeth Lyons, Xlibris
Corporation, 2003

InDeX